THE FAILURE AND THE HOPE

THE FAILURE
AND THE HOPE

Essays of Southern Churchmen

Edited, with an introduction, by

WILL D. CAMPBELL

and

JAMES Y. HOLLOWAY

WILLIAM B. EERDMANS PUBLISHING COMPANY
Grand Rapids, Michigan

All the essays in this collection appeared first, in slightly different form, in *Katallagete—Be Reconciled*, the journal of the Committee of Southern Churchmen, Inc., Box 936, College Station, Berea, Kentucky, 40403. Copyright dates for the individual essays are as follows: Walker Percy, "The Failure and the Hope," © 1965; Thomas Merton, "Events and Pseudo-Events," Will D. Campbell, "Footwashing or the New Hermeneutic?", William Paul Randall, "The Plutocrats and the Po' Folks," Loyal Jones, "Mrs. Combs and the Bulldozers," © 1966; Vincent Harding, "The Gift of Blackness," James Y. Holloway, "Violence and Snopes," © 1967; Beverly Asbury, "Made in the USA," John Howard Griffin, "Take Ten!", Fannie Lou Hamer, "Sick and Tired of Being Sick and Tired," © 1968; Duncan Gray, Jr., "In Defense of the Steeple," Will D. Campbell and James Y. Holloway, "Our Grade Is F," © 1969; James Y. Holloway, "The End of the World," Walker Percy, "Notes for a Novel About the End of the World," Pete Young, "The Rainbow Sign," © 1970; Ann Beard, "Free *Who*?", Will D. Campbell and James Y. Holloway, "An Open Letter to Billy Graham," James G. Branscome, "Annihilating the Hillbilly,"© 1971.

Contents

5

6

PART 4

Foreword

About eight years ago, the Committee of Southern Churchmen began publishing *Katallagete: Be Reconciled.* The name was taken from Paul's letter to the Christians in Corinth. "It is as if God were appealing to you through us: In Christ's name, we implore you, *be reconciled (katallagete)* to God!"

The name had the drawback of being unfamiliar and unpronounceable, but it stuck with us. We were convinced that for too long Christians and the church had blasphemed our mission by identifying evangelism with social action and political programs, selling our birthright, cheaply, for "a piece of the action." To some of us, *katallagete* became a useful reminder that God's reconciliation of all men to himself and to each other is on a different order than the political gimmickry and passion for "relevance" that goes under the name of "social action." It is a reminder that Paul's imperative, *katallagete,* is neither the imperative of moralisms nor a reconciliation to the deceits and slaughters that take place in the world God reconciled in Jesus—the world into which God called Christians into being as his ambassadors. It seems to us that Paul meant, "*Do:* nothing. *Be:* what God makes you in Christ. And in *being,* in Christ, you will find yourself very 'busy.' " As Thomas Merton said it in one of the essays in this volume: "To reconcile man with man and not with God is to reconcile no one at all."

So *Katallagete* stuck with us.

The essays that follow are taken from the past eight years of our journal. They do not constitute, however, "the best of *Katallagete*," because not included are some of our "best" articles: W. H. Ferry's on black colonies and police states, Anthony Towne's on reconciliation, Jacques Ellul's on Cain, William Stringfellow's on double-mindedness and the day of wrath, or essays by Philip and Daniel Berrigan, D. F. Fleming, James Dabbs, Robert Stewart, Vernard Eller, Markus Barth, Julius Lester, Al Ulmer, Jim Douglass, Christopher Lasch, Robert Sherrill, and others. Also not represented is the work of Al Clayton, a member of our editorial board, whose photographs have identified our covers for many years.

The unity of this volume is suggested by the subtitle "Essays of Southern Churchmen." Certainly we claim no special gifts of prophecy because we were born Southerners, or are Southern Christians, or because we still live in the South. On the contrary, we are suspicious about those Southerners who imply that there is a special gift of Southern-ness, a gift that permeates literature, art, politics, life-styles, society, psychology, even Christianity, in a way that makes Southerners better because of these peculiarities. No. It is that we happen to live in the South and we know our region better than we know other ones. And that means, very simply, that we know the particulars of our failures and hopes more intimately than we know the failures and hopes of others.

And that is what these essays are about. They are not "regional." For we are concerned about our failures and hopes as Christians, and they are not unlike the failures and hopes of Christians in New York City, San Diego, Chicago, or Thessalonica, Madras, Rome, or Capernaum. We believe that other Christians will recognize failures and hopes also, if they should happen to hear us talking about ours.

These essays are on a variety of subjects. There is no theological "line" common to them except, perhaps, a distrust of the currents of contemporary, professional theology. If anything unites what follows, it is the confession about the meaning of both "the failure" and "the hope" of Christians at the end of the twentieth century. Our failure as Christians is that we have been seeking reconciliation through social and political action when there already is reconciliation, by God's action, not ours: we are called as Christians only to witness to that action by the being God gives us in Christ. Our failure is that we have sought to be relevant to political and social processes when we should have been challenging these very processes by "the politics of God": and this failure explains why the churches' institutions—congregations, colleges, theologies, seminaries, agencies, boards, etc., etc.—stand by, hapless, but wealthy and respectable, in the face of escalating racism, destruction, and warfare at home and abroad. We have failed because we have sought to be effective in our churchly affairs when all that God has ever asked us to be is faithful, to him in Jesus. We have failed because we have hankered after the approval of the world and so let the world in its darkness and death tell us what the "real" crises in living are all about: that is, we render to Caesar the things that are God's and to God the things that are Caesar's and, like the proud Christians Paul opposed at Corinth, see this as a sign of telling the truth about God. But it is no service to the world to tell it what it already knows and believes and lives and dies for. We have failed as Christians because we have taken theological fads, literary, dramatic and "life"-styles and academic professionalism as more authoritative than the Scriptures. So we have failed because we Christians have announced that "God is dead!" with greater conviction and enthusiasm and clarity than the death-of-God theologians announced it and more emphatically than "godless Communism" ever did.

If this confession of our failures as Christians who live in the South is common to these essays, so also, we believe, is our confession of the hope:

> For the love of Christ leaves us no choice when once we have reached the conclusion that one man died for all and there-fore all mankind has died. His purpose in dying for all was that men, while still in life, should cease to live for them-selves, and should live for him who for their sake died and was raised to life. With us therefore worldly standards have ceased to count in our estimate of any man; even if once they counted in our understanding of Christ, they do so now no longer. When anyone is united to Christ, there is a new world; the old order has gone, and a new order has already begun.
>
> From first to last this has been the work of God. He has reconciled us men to himself through Christ, and he has enlisted us in this service of reconciliation. What I mean is that God was in Christ reconciling the world to himself, no longer holding men's misdeeds against them, and that he has entrusted us with the message of reconciliation. We come therefore as Christ's ambassadors. It is as if God were appeal-ing to you through us: In Christ's name, we implore you, be reconciled to God.

And so we bid you, again, *Katallagete!*

Ad majorem Dei gloriam,

Will D. Campbell

James Y. Holloway

PART 1

1

The Failure and the Hope

WALKER PERCY

Those of us in the South who call ourselves Christians have come face to face with the most critical and paradoxical moment in our history. The crisis is the black revolution. The paradox lies in this: that the hope for the future—and both the hope and the promise, in my opinion and for reasons which shall follow, were never greater—requires as its condition of fulfilment the strictest honesty in assessing the dimensions of our failure.

What lies at issue is whether or not the South will bring to bear its particular tradition and its particular virtues to humanize a national revolution which is in the main secular and which is going to be accomplished willy-nilly with or without the Christian contribution—or whether it will yield the field by default.

The failure of the Christian in the South has been both calamitous and unremarkable. And perhaps that is the

WALKER PERCY's novels include *Love in the Ruins, The Last Gentleman,* and *The Moviegoer,* which received the National Book award in 1962. He is a Catholic layman, a member of the Editorial Board of *Katallagete,* and lives in Covington, Louisiana.

worst of it: that no one finds the failure remarkable, not we who ought to know better, not the victims of our indifference who confess the same Christ, and not even the world who witnessed our failure. No one was surprised. The world which said many years ago, "See how the Christians love one another," would presumably have been surprised if these earlier Christians had violated each other or turned their backs upon the violation. Now as then the children of the world are wiser than the children of light: they witnessed the failure we concealed from ourselves and found it not in the least remarkable.

The world in fact does not think badly of us. It holds us generally speaking to be good, an asset to the community. The sickness of Christendom may lie in fact in this: that we are judged by the world and even to a degree have come to judge ourselves as but one of a number of "groups" or institutions which have a "good" impact on society. One thinks of those panel programs and seminars on educational TV which set out to explore the means of combating juvenile delinquency, crime in the streets, drug addiction and so on. Someone on the panel usually gets around to listing the forces for good in the community which can be enlisted in the battle. There is the home, the schools, the labor unions, the business community; and there are the churches. . . .

And in the matter of racial injustice, the churches are treated with the same respectful impartiality. The media approvingly report the news that such and such a bishop has integrated the parochial schools or that this or that minister has joined a bi-racial committee, in much the same tone with which they report that IBM has set up its own Fair Employment Practices Committee. The bad behavior of Christians is not treated as any worse or more scandalizing than bad behavior anywhere else. When God is invoked by the Klan and the Citizens' Councils, when ministers open the meeting with a prayer; when white Catholics in Louisiana get in fist fights with Negro Catholics on the church steps, nobody cries shame. The world does not laugh and in fact is not even pleased. Because, as everyone knows, churches are, generally speaking, on the list of good institutions and do in fact make valuable contributions to the community—along with the home, the school, the media. . . .

Christians in the South should, of all people, know better. Or perhaps it is more accurate to say that if they don't know better, then Christendom is indeed sick unto death. But in their heart of hearts they do know better. Because the South, more so than the rest of the country, is still Christ-haunted, to use an expression of Flannery O'Connor. Whatever the faults of the South, it is perhaps the only section of the United States where the public and secular consciousness is still to a degree informed by theological habits of thought, the old notions of sin, of heaven and hell, of God's providence, however abused and shopworn these notions may be. Flannery O'Connor, a Catholic novelist, counted it her great good fortune to have been born and raised and to work in the Protestant South. In the Catholic novel she claimed, "the center of meaning will be Christ and the center of destruction will be the devil." The South has always known this, even when its morality was mainly concerned with sex and alcohol to the exclusion of ordinary human cruelty. And the Southerner is apt to inherit, almost despite himself, a theological turn of mind. More likely than not he has grown up in a place drenched in tragedy and memory and to have known firsthand a rich and complex world of human relationships which are marked by a special grace and a special cruelty and guilt.

Our region, I submit, is to a larger degree informed by theological habits of thought than the rest of the country. And those of us who are professing Christians have better reason than most to understand the theological basis and consequences of our actions and less excuse to fall victim to the sociological heresy which sees the church as but one among several "good" institutions which can be used to engineer a democratic society.

It is all the more shameful, then, that the failure is precisely a theological failure. How much more tolerable would have been our position if it had fallen out otherwise, if we could have said to the secular liberals of the Northern cities: yes, it is true that we differ radically from you in our view of the nature of man and the end of man, that we have reservations about your goal of constructing the city of God here and now; further, we don't like some of the things you tolerate in your perfect city. But we applaud your attack on the perennial evils of poverty, inhumanity, and disease; and we too believe that men can be reconciled here and now but that they can only be reconciled through the mediation of God and the love of men for God's sake. We strive for the same goals; we say only that you deceive yourself in imagining that you can achieve these goals without God.

But we can't even say that. The default has occurred on the grounds of our own choosing. The failure has been a failure of love, a violation of that very Mystical Body of Christ which we have made our special property at the risk of scandalizing the world by our foolishness. A scandal has occurred right enough, but it has not been the scandal intended by the Gospels. The failure, that is to say, has occurred within the very order of *sin*, which we have taken so seriously and the world so lightly. Where we have failed worst is not in the sphere of community action wherein little store is set by theological values. Churches indeed have not done at all badly in discharging their sociological functions, combating juvenile delinquency and broken homes and alcoholism. The failure has been rather the continuing and unreflecting cruelty of Christians toward the Negro, the Negro considered not as beloved household pet ("Cruelty? No! Why, I would do anything for Uncle Ned and he for me!") but considered as member of the same Mystical Body, freed and dignified by the same covenant which frees and dignifies us. The sin has been the sin of omission, specifically the Great Southern Sin of Silence. During the past ten years, the first ten years of the black revolution, a good deal was heard about the "good" people of the South, comprising the vast majority, who deplored the violence and who any day would make themselves felt. But these good people are yet to be heard from. If every Christian era has its besetting sin, the medieval church its inquisitional cruelty, eighteenth-century Anglicanism its Laodiceanism, the twentieth-century Christian South might well be remembered by its own peculiar mark: *silence.*

The default of the white Southern Christian was revealed in its proper ironic perspective by the civil rights movement itself. When the good people of the South did not come forward when they were needed, their burden was shouldered by, of all people, the liberal humanist who, like the man St. Paul speaks of in his epistle to the Ephesians, is stranger to every covenant, with no promise to hope for, the world about him and no God—but who nevertheless was his brother's keeper. In the deep South of the 1960s, those who nursed the sick, bound his wounds, taught the ignorant, fed the hungry, went to jail with the imprisoned, were not the Christians of Birmingham or Bogalusa but were, more likely than not, the young CORE professionals or COFO volunteers, Sarah Lawrence sociology majors, agnostic Jewish social workers like Mickey Schwerner, Camus existentialists, and the like.

It is possible for a Southerner to criticize his region in the harshest possible terms, not because he thinks the South is worse than the rest of the country and can only be saved by the Berkeley-Cambridge axis but for the exactly opposite reason: that, in spite of her failures, he suspects that it may very likely fall to the destiny of the South to save the country from the Berkeley-Cambridge axis. If this should prove the case, it is not simply because cities like Los Angeles and New York are exhibiting an almost total paralysis and fecklessness when confronted with Watts and Harlem, while at the same time Atlanta and Greenville are doing comparatively better. (Truthfully, I think the South is "doing better" for an odd mixture of Southern and Northern reasons, none of which has much to do with Christianity; for example, Southern good humor and social grace plus a sharp Yankee eye for the dollar and the "public image.") No, the criticism is leveled and the game is worth the candle because, at least in one Southerner's opinion, the ultimate basis for racial reconciliation must be theological rather than legal and sociological, and in the South, perhaps more than in any other region, the civil and secular consciousness is still sufficiently informed by a theological tradition to provide a sanction for racial reconciliation. (By contrast, the Catholic Church in other parts of the country also provides a powerful sanction, but it is a purely religious sanction and not necessarily reflected in the habitual attitudes of civil bodies such as legislatures and school boards.) The South can, that is, if she wants to. She can just as easily choose the opposite course, like Protestant South Africa.

* * *

The thesis that it may fall to the South to save the Union just as it fell to the North one hundred years ago, might appear not merely paradoxical but in the highest degree fanciful. Yet there are, I believe, good and sufficient reasons for entertaining special hopes for the future, not the least of which is the coming into being of peculiarly Southern groups of Christian churchmen. Like Israel, the South is still killing God's messengers, men like Reeb, Daniel, and Morrisroe, but at least she is killing them and not ignoring them, or worse, conferring upon them lukewarm Civitan honors. And now she may have new prophets.

There are also historical reasons which are largely negative and have to do with the failure of other "good" traditions, traditions which, noble though they might have been and still are, do not perhaps possess the interior resources of renewal which seems to be the perennial and saving gift of Christianity. These failures have cleared the ideological air as it has not been cleared since the first slave came ashore in Virginia. In the failure of old alternatives, future choices become plainer.

The traditions in question and their respective historical difficulties are: (1) the collapse of the old-style "good" white man in the South and the dramatic disintegration of his alliance with the Negro; and (2) the ongoing demoralization of the secular urban-suburban middle-class society, the very culture from which so many of the civil rights activists derive.

The thesis of this article, for which there is not room to lay the proper ground, let alone defend, is that the major ideological source of racial moderation in the South has not been Christian at all but Stoic, that this tradition has now collapsed, that in spite of its nobility (or perhaps because of its nobility) it possessed fatal weaknesses and therefore served as a distracting and confusing alternative to racism, and finally that its collapse has confronted Christians with a crucial test, the outcome of which will be unequivocal triumph or unequivocal disaster. The chips, that is to say, are down and it is time they were.

The degree of reconciliation achieved under this noble and mainly non-Christian ethic was more considerable than is generally realized. As a result of the old "fusion principle," as it was known, the Negro in the deep South enjoyed more civil rights in the period immediately following Reconstruction than at any time afterwards—until the last few years. Restaurants and trains were not segregated. Congressman Catchings of Mississippi, one of the noblest of the Old Redeemers, reported that there were more Negro officeholders in his district than in the entire North. This alliance, it is important to note, was struck between the Negro and the white conservative against the poor whites and the Radical Republicans. It has been this same white conservative leadership which in many parts of the South exerted a more or less consciously moderate racial influence even after it was politically overwhelmed by the latter-day Populist-racists, Vardaman, Heflin, Bilbo, and their followers. The old alliance with the Negro was in part politically motivated. But it also had a strong moral basis. It is the contention here that this morality was paternalistic and Stoic in character and that it derived little or none of its energies from Christian theology. Even in those instances where the best Southern leaders were, like Robert E. Lee, professing Christians, James McBride Dabbs has shown that there was a strong Stoic component in their character formation. Perhaps the most distinguishing mark and, as it turned out, the greatest weakness of the Stoic morality, was its exclusively personal character and its consequent indifference to the social and political commonweal. The Stoic took as his model, either consciously or unconsciously, the emperor Marcus Aurelius, who wrote in his *Meditations*, "Every moment think steadily, as a Roman and a man, to do what thou hast in hand with perfect and simple dignity and a feeling of affection and freedom and justice." Such a moral ideal, lofty as it is, has largely to do with the housekeeping of one's interior castle, specifically the maintenance of its order and the brightness of one's personal honor. In the light of such a code, the doctrine of the Mystical Body of Christ wherein each of us is a member, one of another, and no one is inviolate in the precincts of his soul, must remain incomprehensible.

But it was they, the Stoics, who behaved by their lights

and we who did not. The best of them kept the old broadsword virtues while the Christians by and large egregiously sinned against their own commandments, through commission and omission—in the latter case through an impoverished morality restricted largely to rules for the use of sex and alcohol. It was the Christians in the South who supplied the main ideological support for slavery. It is the Christians now who still underwrite segregation with Levitical quotations and Ham-Shem sociology. Nor is it enough to say that Christ was no social reformer and that St. Paul wasn't worried about freeing slaves. Where the Southern Christian failed was on his own ground, in his own performance in the face of here-and-now cruelty and suffering and inhumanity.

Even when the Christian did come to the aid of the afflicted and abused Negro, he often did so for Stoic reasons, with the old benevolence and the sense of personal bond toward Uncle Ned and Aunt Jemima but without that larger and more mysterious charity which at one and the same time binds men close and sets them free, and does not keep books on gratitude.

Most of us have known the old tradition firsthand and recall it with affection and admiration. I remember in the most vidid way long conversations with my uncle about the plantation system. At that time—in the 1930s—the sharecropper system was coming under heavy attack from "Northern liberals." As a planter, my uncle felt that the attacks were unjust. He believed that the sharecropper system was an outgrowth of a natural partnership between the Confederate veterans who had nothing left but the land and the Negroes who had nothing but their labor. No doubt he was right. To justify its use in modern times, he cited his own experience and that of his friends, who dealt with their tenants more than honorably, serving also as father and friend. To behave with dishonor was to these men a detestable thing, but to mistreat a Negro was unthinkable, precisely because the Negro was helpless. But other men, a great many other men, were not so scrupulous. And the Negro remained helpless, precisely because he had no entity in the public order of things and neither law nor religion felt constrained to underwrite such an entity.

We may speak now of the old tradition without fear of patronizing it, because it was it and not the Christian tradition which fleshed out some of the noblest men this country has produced. We may go even further. As Dabbs wrote in his remarkable book *Who Speaks for the South?*, the final evidence that there was something wrong with the South as a society, that in the last analysis it was not a great society, was that it produced neither saints nor great artists.

Stoic excellence, in short, was not enough. Its code had little relevance in the social and political order. For not only was there the tendency to wash one's hands of prevailing social evils, there was even the temptation to *Schadenfreude*, the peculiar sin of the Stoic, a grim sort of pleasure to be taken in the very deterioration of society, the crashing of the world about one's ears. Southern literature is full of direful, eschatological—and pleasurable—reports of the decline and fall of both the South and the United States.

Though it was defeated politically around 1890, the Stoic tradition has persisted until recently. Nearly everyone in the South has known someone like Atticus Finch in *To Kill a Mockingbird* with his quite Attic sense of decency (and his correspondingly low regard for Christianity) and his courage before the lynch mob. It is, however, this very Stoic tradition which has finally collapsed as a significant influence in the Southern community. The old conservative often became the new conservative, that is, a segregationist and "States' Righter." The force for moderation is now more likely to be the businessman—the "power structure"—the mayor, the manager of the new IBM center or the NASA complex who wants no part of the KKK or the Citizens' Councils, though for reasons which have nothing to do with Christ or with Marcus Aurelius.

The ideological vacuum created by the failure of the gentle tradition has been filled not by Christians but by other elements, the moderate business community and the secular reformer. The Christian clergy has been increasingly active but the inertness of cultural Christendom is well known. Is it possible that this well-known lag between clergy and laity can be traced to still viable Stoic elements in Christendom considered as a cultural artifact which one inherits more or less passively as he inherits language and custom?

There is not much doubt about the existence of such a lag. An increasingly familiar fact of life in the Southern parish, Protestant and Catholic, has come to be the tension between the "radical" new minister or priest and his "conservative" flock. There are the usual grumblings about brainwashing in the seminary. But is this lag to be understood in purely sociopolitical terms of liberal vs. conservative? I think not, because this particular bias has proved quite as refractory to pulpit appeals as to political appeals. I suspect that a good deal of the offense taken can be laid to a fundamental Stoic offense to any demand for public appeal and political morality. There is still the old reflex which somehow rules the preacher out of bounds when he talks about social morality as well as sexual morality. The very man who will get up at all hours to get Ol' Jim out of jail and even risk his life to protect Ol' Jim from the lynch mob is also outraged when Jim's sons demand better schools and better police—not come hat in hand but demand them as ordinary rights of a citizen. And of course the fact is that many of the old-style "good" people, both Christian and Stoic, have now turned against the Negro because of what they deem his "insolence." "If the Negro had not become aggressive," a good Christian man told me the other day,

"I'd still be on his side. It is these demonstrations, his *demanding* rights of me, which changed my attitude." Of *me*? Here is the heart of the matter certainly: it is where the rights are deemed to come from which causes the offense.

Such a response can be traced, I believe, to an antique Southern preoccupation, not with theology, as a rule of social intercourse, but with *manners*. By manners I do not refer in this context to that courtesy which one Christian awards another by virtue of the infinite value he assigns to the other's person but rather to manners understood as a primary concern with an intercourse of gesture, a minuet of overture and response. It is an economy of gesture which in its accounting of debits and credits, of generosity given and gratitude expected, of face and loss of face, is almost Oriental. (Note also the similarities of the classic Stoic tradition with certain Oriental moral philosophies.) A great part of the social intercourse between whites and Negroes in the South, I daresay, was founded on a complex and meticulously observed protocol of manners. And it came to pass that an extraordinary social fabric was woven between black and white using these very elements and in the face of the most trying circumstances. Nor is this to say that this Southern tradition of manners is irrelevant to the problems of the day. It would be a great pity indeed if the ordinary everyday good manners of Southerners, black and white, should be overturned in the present revolution.

But the American Negro today may reply that the social graces of his ancestors in Alabama didn't in the end do him or them much good. It is his present "bad manners" which now offend his old ally—though in all honesty I must admit that the opposite seems the case: the continued "good manners" of the Southern Negro are nothing short of amazing. The point is of course that in a society based largely on an intercourse of manners even the mildest public and political action taken to redress grievances is apt to be received as a code infraction and hence "bad manners."

The old alliance failed through a fatal weakness which now stands revealed. It was based primarily on personal relationships and never really possessed the interior resources, political or religious, through which the integrity of the Negro's person could be guaranteed in its own right.

What is the lesson? The lesson is surely that at the very time the old order has collapsed and new social forces are beginning to stir the South from its long sleep, the Christian laity is still responding with old cultural reflexes to a new and somewhat unmannered order of things. Surely also, the remedy is theological, not merely preaching a gospel of reconciliation, but teaching: setting forth, that is, what is the case as well as what ought to be. What is the case is that the Christian porch is no longer habitable, that pleasant site of cultural Christendom neither quite inside the church nor altogether in the street from which one had the best of both, church on Sundays and at baptism and marriage and death, and the rest of the time lived in the sunny old Stoa of natural grace and good manners. It doesn't work now.

* * *

The Negro in the South has a new ally. He is not the old-style gentleman or Stoic or quasi-Christian but rather the liberal humanist, who is, more likely than not, frankly post-Christian in his beliefs. The clergy has been active in the civil rights movement, sometimes heroically so, but the impetus has not in the main been theological—except among black Southern Christians but even in this case to a decreasing degree, especially among the younger Negroes. Among the volunteers of the Mississippi Summer Project of 1964, it was the exception rather than the rule to come across anyone who had come to Mississippi to implement Christian principles even though the project was sponsored by the National Council of Churches. It was rarer still to find a Southern Christian layman. And yet they were on the whole an earnest and admirable young group.

Here is a point of view, not at all atypical, expressed by one of the volunteers:

> Along with my Core class I teach a religion class at one every afternoon and a class on non-violence at four fifteen. . . . In religion they are being confronted for the first time with people they respect who do not believe in God and with people who do believe in God but who do not take the Bible literally. It's a challenging class because I have no desire to destroy their belief, whether Roman Catholic or Baptist, but I want them to look at things critically and to learn to separate fact from myth in all areas, not just religion.

There is no reason to doubt this statement—that this young person does not wish Baptists and Catholics to lose their faith—though a good deal could be written about the assumptions and begged questions behind the statement. What is noteworthy perhaps is a lack of seriousness, a certain casualness with which the perennially mooted religious questions are assumed to be disposed of. The old animus against the Christian proposition has been replaced by a shrug. Here, at any rate, is the new "good" man, a person of unquestionable goodwill and earnestness who explicitly disavows orthodox Christian belief. She places her confidence, not on the old verities, but on "facts" (that is to say, observable and replicable phenomena) and on social techniques.

This secularization of the civil rights movement has been largely misunderstood in the South. The failure of Southern Christendom has not only been theological—a default in the duty of reconciliation—but prophetic in its blindness both to what happened and what is to come. Confronted by a revolutionary and to a large degree non-Christian movement and obfuscated by his own Stoic reading of race relations—"we have nothing but love for our Negroes and they for us," etc.—the Southern Christian has all too often made the unhappy mistake of labelling the civil rights movement as Communist, immoral, un-American and so on. Apparently there are a few Communists involved and apparently there has been some sexual misbehavior, but this is not an occasion for rejoicing. The reason the Christian racist goes to such lengths to discredit the new allies of the Negro and is so pleased when they uncover sexual sin is not hard to discover. For the bitterest pill for them to swallow is the fact, hardly to be contested and which in his heart he does not contest, that the Negro revolution is mainly justified, mainly peaceful (from the side of the Negroes) and mainly American. For to admit this hard reality would entail *pari passu* a confession of his own failure.

How stands the Christian then *vis-à-vis* the challenge of the new-style "good" man? Better off than before, I think, and less compromised than he was in his relation to the old-style Stoic quasi-Christian gentleman.

The present hope is to be found, paradoxically as it is often the case with Christian hope, in the very extremity of the failure. The old Christian porch, that is to say, is becoming increasingly uninhabitable by moderately serious persons, which is to say our best young people. It is surely not too much to say that if Southern Christendom does not soon demonstrate the relevance of its theology to the single great burning social issues in American life, it runs the risk of becoming ever more what it in fact to a degree already is, the pleasant Sunday lodge of conservative Southern businessmen which offends no one and which no one takes seriously.

The larger hope and opportunity of the Christian gospel lies of course in the terrible dilemma of the new "good" man himself, the denizen, we might call him, of the victorious technological-democratic society. A great

28

deal has been written about him and his twentieth-century sickness. Suffice it here to say only what he has said about himself: that the very urban and middle-class society from which have come so many of the earnest young revolutionaries is itself marked by the malaise and anomie and other symptoms of the new sickness. There is nothing new in this. Indeed preachers speak every Sunday about the emptiness of modern man and the One who can fill the emptiness. And they are right. But God help us here in the South (or in Chicago or Los Angeles) if we imagine that reconciliation is not our business here and now and that all we have to do is convert the Communists and bring Christ to the "empty modern man." Because these latter are not going to be listening. The fruits, by which they had every right to know us, were too meagre.

2

"Made in the USA"

BEVERLY A. ASBURY

> He said therefore to the multitudes that came out to be baptized by him, "You brood of vipers! Who warned you to flee from the wrath to come? Bear fruits that befit repentance, and do not begin to say to yourselves, 'We have Abraham as our father'; for I tell you, God is able from these stones to raise up children to Abraham. Even now the axe is laid to the root of the trees; every tree therefore that does not bear fruit is cut down and thrown into the fire."
>
> Luke 3:7-9

> The word that came to Jeremiah from the Lord: "Stand in the gate of the Lord's house, and proclaim there this word, and say, Hear the word of the Lord, all you men of Judah who enter these gates to worship the Lord. Thus says the Lord of hosts, the God of Israel, Amend your ways and your doings, and I will let you dwell in this place. Do not trust in these deceptive words: 'This is the temple of the Lord, the temple of the Lord, the temple of the Lord.' For if you truly amend your ways and your doings, if you truly execute

BEVERLY A. ASBURY is University Chaplain, Vanderbilt University, and a board member of the Committee of Southern Churchmen.

justice one with another, if you do not oppress the alien, the fatherless or the widow, or shed innocent blood in this place, and if you do not go after other gods to your own hurt, then I will let you dwell in this place, in the land that I gave of old to your fathers forever. Behold, you trust in deceptive words to no avail. Will you steal, murder, commit adultery, swear falsely, burn incense to Ba'al, and go after other gods that you have not known, and then come and stand before me in this house, which is called by my name, and say, 'We are delivered!'—only to go on doing all these abominations? Has this house, which is called by my name, become a den of robbers in your eyes? Behold, I myself have seen it, says the Lord."

Jeremiah 7:1-11

John Sorace is an Assistant Chief of Police in Nashville. Last fall he testified before Senator McClellan's Permanent Investigations subcommittee that black college students in Nashville were teaching Negro children to "hate" white people. Chief Sorace singled out for attack the "Liberation School" organized by the Student Nonviolent Coordinating Committee and St. Anselm's Episcopal Church in North Nashville.

The "Liberation School," he testified, was a "hate whitey" school. The Chief carried his point, for the school was closed and St. Anselm's pastor, Father James Woodruff, a Negro, was subsequently transferred out of Nashville by his ecclesiastical superiors. Moreover, Chief Sorace successfully mobilized powers and people in Nashville against the use of "federal" money to support what he described as the teaching of "hate whitey."

Now how many of us can believe in our hearts that any black man in America needs to be *taught* to "hate whitey"? Blacks do not have to be taught *that*, at least not in school! Negroes, Blacks, Afro-Americans learn to hate us white men from us—from the way we conduct ourselves, from our habits and actions and attitudes to-

ward them. As for "federal" money being used in programs to teach "hate" of one race by another, shouldn't
we white men recall what we were taught during our
school days about "colored people," or more to the
point, do we dare forget the clever but equally invidious
and effective cruelties played out against black children
in the schools we whites have so desperately sought to
"integrate" with black children—using "federal" money?

                        * * *

   Now would you believe that one of Nashville's leading
newspapers recently reported as a front-page story that
Stokely Carmichael was "seen in town"? Would you
believe that a student at Tennessee State looks like Stokely, and that *he* was the subject of the front-page story,
not Stokely? Would you believe what this Tennessee
State student alleges: that he and a friend were picked up
at gunpoint and detained by the Nashville police for four
hours? That they were never charged with a crime? That
they were never allowed to telephone an attorney? That
one Assistant Chief of Police allegedly gave them a lecture on how Negroes should behave in Nashville, telling
one of them to get rid of his Afro-cut because "Black
Power advocates" used it, and "Black Power advocates"
were trying to take over the country and give it to "the
Communists"?
   Would you believe that in a recent search for the
murderer of a policeman, black citizens have charged that
their apartments were raided and men interrogated but
no warrants were issued for the search and that no one
was charged with any crime? Would you believe that no
Nashville daily newspaper exposed these alleged violations of law and order, of civil liberties and human
dignity—although one of them is called a liberal paper?
Would you believe that these events could happen in any
white man's part of town? Do you believe that a daily

newspaper—"liberal" or "conservative"—would have ignored these events had white men been treated in this
manner?

So who needs a *school* to teach black men to hate
"whitey"? We whites say with all seriousness: "if 'they'
were all like Perry," the first Negro in SEC basketball
competition. But what we mean is that Perry is "smart,
good looking, athletic, clean. He dresses well. Yes sir!
Perry's almost 'white!' " That does not mean, of course,
that Perry *is* that way. Perry may well not be what we
think he is. And if he ever was, he has changed—as a
result of his experience in this city. Perry now refuses to
go where other black students cannot go. He refuses to be
"accepted" by us when other black students are *not*
"accepted." We like to think that Perry is "white like
us," but Perry won't go. That is why he is in an
Afro-American Club at good old Vanderbilt University.
And there are many like him. They refuse our white
terms. They are no longer interested in what we "offer."
Whenever we think that "our" black students are bitter
and cynical, let us at least have the intellectual integrity,
if not the moral resource, to admit that they did not have
to go to school to get that way. It is "Made in the USA."

* * *

What about Nat Turner? They taught about Nat in the
"Liberation School" in North Nashville—the one closed
by Chief Sorace's testimony, the one that Father Woodruff defended until he, too, was moved on. William
Styron has written a novel, *The Confessions of Nat Turner*, recording one white man's impressions of Turner, a
black slave who in 1831 led a sustained and bloody revolt
against white men in southeastern Virginia. *We* were not
taught about Nat Turner's rebellion in our history
classes—even in our self-satisfied liberal arts colleges, in
the North or South—because after one hundred and fifty

years we still cannot face what that rebellion symbolizes. It has never been true that all black men were "Sambo" types, so brainwashed and brutalized by slavery as to be incapable of revolt. (Our magnolia-scented Departments of English, so proud and serious about Faulkner, could have told us that—if they had been willing to face up to what Nat Turner meant.) Nat Turner led a revolt that murdered more than a score of white people; he and his band were called "ferocious miscreants" by white contemporaries. But black men see in Nat a victim of hatred: a man taught hatred by slavery in the United States. Nat Turner was made in the USA. His people came from Africa, but we white people and our system made him what he was. His hatred was produced in America. We may have produced "Sambos" who were psychologically incapable of revolt, but Nat could, and did, and that is why black men today teach about him. Who can blame them?

Some have argued that Nat Turner's rebellion may have prevented Virginia from becoming a free state and remaining in the Union. And that this in turn may have prevented a more satisfactory resolution of slavery than the one provided by the Civil War. Reconstruction, and segregation. And today it is being said that the riots in the urban ghettos are setting back the "cause" of civil rights: that violence defeats any hope of improving the conditions of ghetto life. Blame it on Nat. Blame it on Stokely. Blame it on Rap. Blame it on Malcolm X. Blame it on Black Power. And miss the real issue: the *cause* of violence, the *source* of it in America today.

Violence is not the real issue. The *cause* of the violence is. The President of the United States is wrong when he suggests that "crime in the streets" is the real issue. The *cause* of crime is! We shall see, Congressmen, if riots cease after you make it illegal to cross state lines with the "intention" of inciting violence. Imprison Rap, and see what is improved. Deport Stokely, and see if crime and

turmoil disappear. Demand law and order, and watch for
the results. Murder Malcolm and see what has been
ended—Watts, Detroit, Newark, Nashville?

Rap Brown was made in the USA, just as Nat Turner
was. And the man who saw this most clearly and artic-
ulated it most precisely was Malcolm X. *The Autobiography of Malcolm X* belongs on the "must" list of every
white man's reading. In Malcolm we see Nat, Rap,
Stokely, the Afro-Americans, and every so-called black
"extremist" in America today. We understand how they
are "Made in the USA" and how they feel about it. Most
important of all, we begin to understand ourselves because we also are "Made in the USA"—white men, white
Christians, white American Christians. We learn something of what that means from Malcolm. It hurts, but it
may help to heal.

Malcolm was made in the USA, a product, as most of
the "militant" black leaders today, of Northern integration. His autobiography and his speeches reveal how
keen was his insight, how prophetic his words and convictions, about racism, about integration, about the North
and South of the United States. But Malcolm did not end
his career as a product of hatred made in the USA,
because he never stopped hating the system that brutalized and degraded the black man. Malcolm had an un-
compromising honesty and integrity. He learned the history of black men and the genetic history of white men.
He freed himself of the white notion that "black-equals-
bad-and-ugly." He exposed the perversions of Western
history and religion. He called attention to the obvious
fact—of which little is made in lily-white Christian "seminaries"—that Jesus and Paul were Hebrews—dark and
swarthy Jews, perhaps even black, as some of the early
Hebrews were. At one stage in his life, Malcolm believed
that white men were "devils," because of what he knew
of "the enormity, the horrors, of the so-called *Christian*

white man's crime. . . ." Later, after a journey to Mecca,
he altered his generalizations about all white men, but he
would never buy the white, blue-eyed, blond-bearded
Jesus of our white chapels and Sunday schools, urging
black men to accept their fate until they died and entered
"some dreamy heaven-in-the-hereafter. . . ." Indeed, he
found the best "fishing" for Muslims among storefront
Christians.

And why not? Listen to what Malcolm and Mr.
Muhammad have said about Christians, and hear the *truth*
(even the truth of the gospel) in their words:

> Christianity is the white man's religion. The Holy Bible in the
> white man's hands and his interpretations of it have been the
> greatest single ideological weapon for enslaving millions of
> non-white human beings. Every country the white man has
> conquered with his guns, he has always paved the way, and
> salved his conscience, by carrying the Bible and interpreting
> it to call the people "heathens" and "pagans"; then he sends
> his guns, then his missionaries behind the guns to mop
> up. . . . The *ignorance* we black race here in America have,
> and the *self-hatred* we have, they are fine examples of what
> the white slavemaster has seen fit to teach to us. Do we show
> the plain common sense, like every other people on this
> planet Earth, to unite among ourselves? No! We are humbling
> ourselves, sitting-in, and begging-in, trying to *unite* with the
> slavemaster! I don't seem able to imagine any more ridicu-
> lous sight. A thousand ways every day, the white man is
> telling you "You can't live here, you can't enter here, you
> can't eat here, drink here, walk here, work here, you can't
> ride here, you can't play here, you can't study here." Haven't
> we yet seen enough to see that he has no plan to *unite* with
> you?
>
> You have tilled his fields! Cooked his food! Washed his
> clothes! You have cared for his wife and children when he
> was away. In many cases, you have even suckled him at your
> breast! You have been far and away better Christians than
> this slavemaster who *taught* you his Christianity!

You have sweated blood to help him build a country so rich that he can today afford to give away millions—even to his *enemies!* And when those enemies have gotten enough from him to then be able to attack him, you have been his brave soldiers, *dying* for him. And you have been always his most faithful servant during the so-called "peaceful" times—

And, *still,* this Christian American white man has not got it in him to find the human *decency,* and enough sense of *justice,* to recognize us, and accept us, the black people who have done so much for him, as fellow human beings!

In equally militant terms, Malcolm rejected integration:

The word "integration" was invented by a Northern liberal. The word has no real meaning. I ask you: in the racial sense in which it's used so much today, whatever "integration" is supposed to mean, can it precisely be defined? The truth is that "integration" is an *image,* it's a foxy Northern liberal's smokescreen that confuses the true wants of the American black man. Here in these fifty racist and neo-racist states of North America, this word "integration" has millions of white people confused, and angry, believing wrongly that the black masses want to live mixed up with the white man. That is the case only with the relative handful of those "integration"-mad Negroes. I'm talking about those "token-integrated" Negroes who flee from their poor, down-trodden black brothers—from their own self-hate, which is what they're really trying to escape. I'm talking about these Negroes you will see who can't get enough of nuzzling up to the white man. These "chosen few" Negroes are more white-minded, more anti-black, than even the white man is.

Human rights! Respect as *human beings!* That's what America's black masses want. That's the true problem. The black masses want not to be shrunk from as though they are plague-ridden. They want not to be walled up in slums, in the ghettoes, like animals. They want to live in an open, free society where they can walk with their heads up, like men, and women!

Toward the end of his life Malcolm made his famous journey to Mecca. Subsequently, he said:

> In the past, yes, I have made sweeping indictments of *all* white people. I never will be guilty of that again—as I know now that some white people *are* truly sincere, that some truly are capable of being brotherly toward a black man. The true Islam has shown me that a blanket indictment of all white people is as wrong as when whites make blanket indictments against blacks. . . .

> It was in the Holy World that my attitude was changed, by what I experienced there, and by what I witnessed there, in terms of brotherhood. . . . And now that I am back in America, my attitude here concerning white people has to be governed by what my black brothers and I experience here, and what we witness here—in terms of brotherhood. The *problem* here in America is that we meet such a small minority of individual so-called "good," or "brotherly" white people. Here in the United States, notwithstanding those few "good" white people, it is the *collective* 150 million white people whom the *collective* 22 million black people have to deal with!

> Why, here in America, the seeds of racism are so deeply rooted in the white people collectively, their belief that they are "superior" in some way is so deeply rooted, that these things are in the national white subconsciousness. Many whites are even actually unaware of their own racism, until they face some test, and then their racism emerges in one form or another.

> Listen! The white man's racism toward the black man here in America is what has got him in such trouble all over the world, with other non-white peoples. The white man can't separate himself from the stigma that he automatically feels about anyone, no matter who, who is not his color. And the non-white peoples of the world are sick of the condescending white man! That's why you've got all this trouble in places like Viet Nam.

Malcolm, like Nat, Rap, Stokely, was "Made in the USA." Malcolm had to be reborn in Mecca to move beyond hatred of white men. In that move lies the real moral of this essay. Everything else is prelude. There is no gospel, no *good* news, until we face this. We have to look at what white America has made. We have to look in the face and eyes of Nat, Rap, Stokely and Malcolm and hear what they said. Here are some words from Malcolm about repentance:

> Are you aware that some Protestant theologians, in their writings, are using the phrase "post-Christian era"—and they mean *now*. And what is the greatest single reason for this Christian church's failure? It is its failure to combat racism. It is the old "You sow, you reap" story. The Christian Church sowed racism—blasphemously; now it reaps racism. Sunday mornings in this year of grace 1965, imagine the "Christian conscience" of congregations guarded by deacons barring the door to black would-be worshipers, telling them "You can't enter *this* House of God!"

> Tell me, if you can, a sadder irony than that St. Augustine, Florida—a city named for the black African saint who saved Catholicism from heresy—was recently the scene of bloody race riots.

> I believe that God now is giving the world's so-called "Christian" white society its last opportunity to repent and atone for the crimes of exploiting and enslaving the world's non-white peoples. It is exactly as when God gave Pharaoh a chance to repent. But Pharaoh persisted in his refusal to give justice to those whom he oppressed. And, we know, God finally destroyed Pharaoh.

> Is white America really sorry for her crimes against the black people? Does white America have the capacity to repent—and to atone? Does the capacity to repent, to atone, exist in a majority, in one-half, in even one-third of American white society?

Many black men, the victims—in fact most black men—would like to be able to forgive, to forget, the crimes.

But most American white people seem not to have it in them to make any serious atonement—to do justice to the black man. Indeed, how *can* white society atone for enslaving, for raping, for unmanning, for otherwise brutalizing *millions* of human beings, for centuries? What atonement would the God of Justice demand for the robbery of the black people's labor, their lives, their true identities, their culture, their history—and even their human dignity?

A desegregated cup of coffee, a theater, public toilets—the whole range of hypocritical "integration"—these are not atonement.

* * *

Has white America repented for our racist crimes? Are we willing to alter the course of what we have done? Do we have the capacity to repent, to turn—and to atone for what we have done? Jeremiah called his people to stop being defensive, to stop hiding behind legalities. He called for men to write the law of God in their hearts, to change their attitudes, habits, feelings, and actions. His people condemned him, but Jeremiah knew that apart from repentance men would die from the inside out. And John the Baptist came preaching repentance in the wilderness. He called the good religious people a band of snakes, trying to flee God's wrath on their deeds. He warned that there was no escape—only repentance. Without repentance, only doom. Without repentance, no good news. "Even now the ax is laid to the root of the trees; every tree therefore that does not bear good fruit is cut down and thrown into the fire." And Jesus went to *that* very preacher to be baptized. The message of repentance received his sanction. As he was to die for man so he repented in the name of man.

"White Christian, listen!" When we see Nat, Rap, and Malcolm; when we face our part in making them; when we face our guilt and complicity, what shall we *do?* What *can* we do? Nothing. Nothing but "repent"—and that is not in our hands, but God's. But we can, as John said, "bear fruit that befits repentance"! It is not what we do that is crucial, anyway. It is what we become. There is *no* program of action that alone can solve things. There is *no* escape from what we have sowed. No war on poverty, no matter how adequately financed and seriously administered, will do it. That won't change *us.* That won't affect the racism of white society. We have to bring fruits that befit repentance as Christians, and as a Christian community. Repentance has to do with us individually and collectively.

We can bear some gifts that God may accept, and turn us, repent us, from our wickedness. We can stop being "segregationists" and become men. We can stop being "integrationists" and become human. We can fight against the collective manifestations that imprison men. We can quit the ridiculous business of being "liberals" and "conservatives," judging one another as wrong or dangerous. We can start by repenting of labels and becoming human beings. How can one be "liberal" or "conservative" about *human* rights? He can only be human if he knows that he and every other man is a child of God. Let us bear fruit that befits repentance and become *human* and create a community in which full humanity is possible for everyone. We can lay aside our clichés and stereotypes and risk getting some experiences with other human beings. We can stop compromising and pussy-footing and deceiving one another about *human* rights. We can face the fact that our nation and our people are being destroyed from within. We can put human lives—in the ghettos and Deltas of Mississippi and Vietnam—above the preservation of *any* institution, church, or college. We can demand that the church preach and practice a message rooted in the faith that God made of one blood all the men of the earth to dwell together. We can follow one who dwelt in human form to break down all the barriers and walls between men. We can move to restructure our society—not for integration but for full human community.

What *can* a white Christian do? He can stop calling Stokely a racist, and acknowledge that white racism in America made Stokely and Rap. What can a white student do? He can recognize that the real battle line for him is in his own home community, among his own fellow whites, in the white political system. He can stop defending unworthy practices: he can refuse to go any place not open in fact and in spirit to another human being because he is black. He can do that, even and especially if it means a church, a fraternity, a country club. He can reject those forms of subtle racism he knows so well in his heart. He can attempt to show a road to full human rights and dignity to all men. He *can* pay that price.

Even if it is too late in our history to bear fruits that will turn off the racial hatred and warfare—and it is too late for Nat and Stokely and Rap and millions more—it is never too late to be faithful to what God did for all men in Christ. That, after all, is the sum of the gospel. It is never too late to hold to the promises of God, that repentance and atonement are God's good news to all men, about man! That in repentance is reconciliation: not slavery but freedom, not many races but one mankind. The life given by God to *all men* in Jesus Christ lies not in death but life—and that abundantly.

So be it! So be it!

3

"Take Ten!"

JOHN HOWARD GRIFFIN

I am a man who is white, sitting in a meeting among men who are black. A young man speaks. Only occasionally does he address me directly.

"Take ten," he calls out.

"Take ten," the others intone.

"Take twenty. Thirty's better—make up for somebody that can't get his ten."

Whether the meetings are held in Kansas, California, New Jersey, or Michigan, the liturgy is similar. "Take ten."

Young men call it out in jovial voices, on the streets, in the supermarkets. "Take ten!" The white world thinks they mean "take a ten-minute break."

They don't. They mean there are ten whites for every

JOHN HOWARD GRIFFIN is a novelist, photographer, and essayist who lives in Fort Worth, Texas. In 1964 he was co-recipient of the Pope John XXIII *Pacem in Terris* award; his *Black Like Me* received the Ainsfield Wolf award from *Saturday Review* in 1961. He is presently completing a biography of Thomas Merton, and is a member of the Committee of Southern Churchmen.

black and before the whites kill the blacks each black should take ten whites with him.

A black man, middle-aged, well-dressed, a minister, leans to me and whispers: "You'd better listen. They're the ones that are calling the plays. They're saying it. You listen."

"Does the white American love the Nazis? He acts like it. The Nazis killed six million Jews. The Jews didn't know what was happening to them. They didn't raise a finger. Well—*fool!*—do you think we're going to go like that? Do you think we don't know? We're going to take ten."

"Amen, brother," the others call out.

"Hell! Let's stop resisting the draft. Let them send us to Vietnam. Only when we get there, let's not shoot that yellow man out front. We can take our ten right there alongside us."

Silence.

"The snipers have been told not to hit anybody. We haven't wanted to hurt the white individual—just the power structure. Now some big fat white-ass mayors are telling their police and the guard to shoot to kill. Now our snipers are going to shoot to kill. Any town where the white leaders want to exterminate us—and that's all it is, just extermination—there's where we've got to shoot to kill and each of us take ten or twenty."

"Amen. . . ."

"They can't say we haven't tried every other way."

The older men, the well-dressed older men added their *amens* to that.

"Now this is the *only* way left. They talking about us *deprived*. Hell, I go to college. I was holding down two jobs when they picked me up. Yeah, they picked me up. I didn't have anything but a stick and a stone on me. They beat me on the way to jail. They sprayed insect repellent in my eyes. They messed up my wrist, and all the time they were saying 'You ain't hurt, nigger, Bop! You all right. Bop! You all right. Bop!' Then the next day they released the white fellow who was down in our area shooting up the houses—turned him out on a one thousand dollar bond, not a scratch on him either. And they let me out on a *five* thousand dollar bond—and don't you know they told me to go and be good!"

"Sure. Sure," the others said.

"And no white man—no church group—nobody said a thing. They don't care."

* * *

I have been attending these meetings all over this land, listening, mute.

I am asked: "What do you say to such young men?"

I don't say anything. I listen. What can you say? An older, burned-out black man said to me not long ago when he took me into one of these meetings: "If you have to talk, don't say anything pious. We can't stand to hear the white man say another pious word."

What words are there to speak to a young man who tells me in an agonized voice: "A year ago I knew right from wrong. They treated me like a mad dog. Now, I'm sorry to say it, but if I walk into some supermarket and just one man or woman looks at me that certain way, or calls me 'boy' or 'nigger,' then I'm going to fix him so he can't see the sky. A year ago the thought of killing *any* man would make me shake all over and want to vomit. Now I'd kill him and then I'd just mosey back to the pool hall—it's the only *goddam* place we got to go—and my hand wouldn't even shake when I put that eight ball in the side pocket."

These meetings are not few, they are many. And they are attended not only by the young, but also by older men, even by prominent older men who have finally been driven to give up any hope that the white man will ever see, will ever act in good faith. One point is seldom understood by whites: most Negroes hate the solutions to which the "white structure" drives men. Negroes don't want this to happen but the pressures pile up. Negroes think whites are blind not to see the total triumph of the white racists.

Whenever a disturbance occurs, it is automatically assumed in the white press, the white community, the white Congress that it has been set off by Negroes, probably by "outside agitators who come in and stir up the good local Negroes." But a quite different pattern is emerging, one already well known to Negroes. In many riot areas the patterns are almost identical. Usually late in the evening, city officials will be warned that a neighboring community has been reduced to flames and that carloads of Negroes are converging from that neighboring area to destroy the city or town. The leaders prepare without checking because the warning always comes late, the danger is immediate. Riot controls are put into effect. The white community arms itself. This has happened in many widely diverse areas: it was the pattern in Mansfield, Texas (Northside Fort Worth reputed to be in flames); in Wichita (Kansas City in flames and 250 carloads of armed Negroes coming to destroy Wichita); in Cedar Rapids (Des Moines in flames, etc.). In some cities panic is intensified with rumors of atrocities: a white lad has just been castrated by two Negroes, though the white lad is never named or placed in evidence. The police, the guard, armed and under tension, prepare to face the "enemy." All it takes then is for a few men to drive through the Negro community shooting off guns or stoning houses. Negroes pour out, sometimes as in Wichita, only with stones and sticks. They are picked up, unjustly they feel, and the "riot" is on. Negroes believe, and so do I, that white racists trigger these holocausts; but from the white "investigators" and press, the same story emerges: sedition, the whole thing was carefully planned within the heart of the Negro community. This is only one of the reasons Negroes feel that white racism is triumphant and that Negroes don't really have a chance anyway, so why not take the whole thing with them, leave the whites nothing.

Men who consider themselves "good whites" remain silent in such areas, often because they do not perceive the patterns (which seems suspicious, indeed incomprehensible, to most Negroes). The silence—no matter what the cause—is viewed as a condoning silence by Negroes.

Negroes have meetings where outraged victims speak to the chorus of *amens*. Parents sit silent while their sons show their scars. The white man will break all the laws in the book to keep Negroes down, they say. The white man thinks we are fools. The white man's crimes against us go unpunished. Mountains of evidence pile up. The churches are silent. The schools send white-assed sociologists. We ask for bread and the white man feeds us a committee. We *demand* justice and we get a committee. Self-determination, God, the white man even has a committee to see how much self-determination *he's* going to give *us*. It vomits out. Sedition? "You drive us crazy," Dr. Nathan Wright said, "and then when we act crazy you call it sedition."

At the end of one such meeting, a young man, his eyes glazed with terminal agony, said quietly, "You go and tell your nonviolent Negro friend and you go and tell your friend Mr. Jesus Christ: shit." The last word whispered in the deepest despair I have ever heard from a human voice.

That evening I went back into the white world and gave a lecture and heard the questions asked by white men, good white men, sincere and troubled white men. And I wished that there were no Negroes in my audience because the questions asked by good white men now often drive Negroes into a frenzy.

A young minister stood up. "Well, Mr. Griffin, you have presented the problem very well, but I would like to have your ideas on what we, as Christians, can do to help?"

A Negro man, a national director of NAACP, sat on the stage beside me. I saw his hands knot and heard him whisper, "Christ."

After that meeting, which the Negro man and I had both attended in the afternoon, the question that made sense to the minister sounded strangely irrelevant to us. I could almost hear the groans of Negroes in the audience. I felt like saying: "Form a committee." I felt like giving him Thomas Merton's answer: "Before you do a damned thing, just *be* what you say you are, a Christian: then no one will have to tell you what to do. You'll know."

Instead, I gave him an even poorer answer: "You ask what we, as Christians, can do? First we have to recognize that we *didn't*. There isn't any time left to start. But we are still obligated to go on and act as though there were. We still hear the voice of outrage over the actions of black men. We still do not hear any similar outcry from Christians or others against racist crimes."

I left it there, not a good answer, feeling that almost any answer was as irrelevant as the question had seemed. How could I make the young minister taste the fetor that poured out of a brilliant young Negro who told me this: "When those of you who profess to be God-centered show the kind of passionate concern over God's presence that I feel over his absence in your white institutions, then you won't have to salvage men like me."

Realistically, we must encourage every effort of solution, all in seeing clearly that racism can easily triumph and that only afterward will we be horrified enough to wonder how a nation could have let itself be led into allowing conflict and fratricide to win over the powers of reconciliation. Some of us must document the tragedy so that at least we will not lie to history, and we must go on acting as though we had a chance, all in seeing the lines of conflict and fratricide grow stronger. Some of us must do this even though we are filled with a terrible nausea before the task.

4

The Gift of Blackness

VINCENT HARDING

> There are varieties of gifts, but the same Spirit. There are varieties of service, but the same Lord. There are many forms of work, but all of them, in all men, are the work of the same God. In each of us the Spirit is manifested in one particular way, for some useful purpose. One man, through the Spirit, has the gift of wise speech, while another, by the power of the same Spirit, can put the deepest knowledge into words. Another, by the same Spirit, is granted faith; another, by the one Spirit, gifts of hearing, and other miraculous powers; another has the gift of prophecy, and another ability to distinguish true spirits from false; yet another has the gift of ecstatic utterance of different kinds, and another the ability to interpret it. But all these gifts are the work of one and the same Spirit, distributing them separately to each individual at will.
>
> I Corinthians 12:4-11

VINCENT HARDING, a writer and historian, is Director of The Institute of The Black World, Atlanta, Georgia. He has taught at Spelman College and has lectured at universities and at conferences throughout the United States. During the 1960s he was director of the Mennonite House in Atlanta. He is a board member of the Committee of Southern Churchmen.

There is a sense in which this message is still being shaped within me. In a sense it is a part of my reflections (particularly insistent over the last year and a half) on the meaning of what it is to be black and American and an historian—and at the same time to be caught in the Jesus bag. So there is something that will be necessarily incomplete in what I am trying to say, and something, I am sure, that will at times be quite incoherent. Nevertheless, the jagged edges of the inner mystery that is roaring about has been ripping at my own guts in such a way that it seems right that I should try to begin by getting some of this out, for my own benefit and perhaps for others. Because of the tenuousness and the tentativeness of all this, it might be good for us to begin by praying both for you and for me: *Come by here, my Lord, come by here; we all need you, Lord, come by here.*

Part of the text for what I want to try to say is located in Paul's message to the church of Corinth. In that sense it's a conventional kind of setting for a sermon. But part of the text for these groping words would require a rhythm-blues combo, with Aretha Franklin or Ray Charles. For much of what I am aching to say grows out of the blues experience, which in itself has grown out of my experience and the experiences of a lot of other people who look like me. So a section of the text would have to be something like those two blues lyrics that Ellison played on so well in his *Invisible Man*, one of them out of the songs of Louis Armstrong: "What did I do to be so black and blue?" The other would be the blues that Ellison made up as he was going along: "Bread and wine, bread and wine, your cross ain't nearly so heavy as mine."

This section of the text is also to be found in the words of one of today's better young black writers who is producing some beautiful things to be read and heard, a young man named Ronald Fair who grew up in Chicago and is now living in Mexico. In an article recently published in *Negro Digest,* Ronald Fair closed with these words, "God, it must be terrible not to be born black in this day and age." What I'd like to suggest at the outset is that the text that begins with Louis Armstrong's words, "What did I do to be so black and blue?" and ends with Ronald Fair's affirmation of the tremendous meaning of being black in this age is not simply an exercise in dialectic. Rather it represents a significant forward movement and a shifting, a shifting in the understanding of the essence of the black experience in America. Something has happened between Louis Armstrong's tough moaning in the 1920s and Ronald Fair's bold statement in 1967. And I think that what has happened might be spoken of, to use the biblical context, as the growing recognition by Afro-Americans of the possibility that within the heart of our blackness there is a gift, a gift in the most marvelous biblical sense of the word. Not the pleasant, pointless, painless, tinsel-wrapped experience that we think of when we think of gifts, nor the romanticized gifts claimed by so many oppressed people to relieve the deadliness of their existence. Rather, when I speak of a gift being at the heart of blackness in this land, I speak of gift in terms of the tough, hammered-out, often brutal experience which nevertheless produces a new reality, a new reality that may benefit the entire society and the entire world—to say nothing of the benefit it might bring to those who call themselves the church. This is why I began with the context of Paul's words about the gifts that had been granted to the people of God for the benefit of them all and for the benefit of the world.

I should like to spend some time just looking at a few of the kinds of gifts that Paul was referring to in this letter, such as the gift that he called the gift of faith, the gift that he called the capacity to distinguish between false spirits and true, the gift of prophecy, the gift of— not love—I do not want to use that word since it is so suspect in these days. Perhaps, we could say the gift of compassion; and finally the gift of healing.

* * *

Now what I am suggesting is that there is a sense in which the gift of blackness in this land, in this strange, white—almost white—land is a gift that encompasses all of these gifts. For instance, the gift of faith: It should be clear to anyone who has taken the time to examine the shape of the black experience in America that there is a sense in which we who are descendants of slaves could not be existing today in the midst of the American madness if there were not some kind of gift of faith. We have talked about it in conventional terms before. We have discovered this gift of faith in those songs of faith that came out of the depths of our suffering, songs that represent a tremendous insight into the meaning of the human experience. These are songs represented by words like, "Nobody knows the troubles I've seen, Glory Hallelujah." What kind of madness is that? "Nobody knows the troubles I've seen, *Glory Hallelujah*!" Obviously this is speaking of the gift of faith, a faith that suggests that it is only in the midst of troubles like nobody has seen that there can develop some sense of the true meaning of the glory of the human existence. I think that this is part of the meaning of our gift, the gift that has made it possible for us to continue. We have also made many references in times past to another aspect of the gift that we call faith. It was faith in the coming of the deliverer, sometimes expressed in songs like, "Go down, Moses, way down in Egypt-land, tell old Pharaoh to let my people go." This has been part of the Negro hope in America as long as there have been black people here. We believed in the night that there would be Moses who would say, "Let my black people go." Go *where*, we were not always sure. Go *how*, we did not know, but, go. Surely it took a certain kind of gift of faith to believe this, to trust that this might actually happen.

* * *

But I would like to suggest that there is another kind of faith that has been operative, especially as black people moved out of the heart of the Southern experience and left the environs of the rural areas to explore the hard strangeness of the Northern cities. After we had moved out of the South, and after many of us had deserted the old churches, we could no longer sing about heaven because we didn't really believe in it any more, and we could no longer sing about the hopes of the North because we had been there and all of our hopes there had been crushed.

Still, there was faith. Out of that experience of moving with the trains and moving with the migrations and moving to the North to the hopelessness and the strangeness and the sadness, there was yet a tough faith that gave us a capacity to endure in the midst of all of this. It gave us a capacity to endure and to produce a literature—in the blues—which surely must be called a kind of proto-existentialism. For if there was ever any situation in which people could say, "Hell is your neighbor," black people in America have known this. If there was ever a group of people who could say, "Life is an absurd existence with no exit," black people in America, especially once we got North, could say this. Then in the midst of this saying and in the fire of this experience, we began to sing again some kind of strange faith that was trying to say what it meant to live where there was no exit and the white neighbors were indeed the agents of hell. Out of this came the blues. The blues was our statement of faith, strange faith, sometimes convoluted faith, sometimes pointless faith, but still faith. And the blues said, "feeling tomorrow just like I feel today," somehow knowing that tomorrow was going to bring nothing more than what was being experienced in a thousand bitter todays. Somehow it seems to me that this kind of experience—the experience of living in a situation that can be described only as absurd, and yet having the faith to continue reaching into that situation and looking for some means by which to endure—that this could not have happened without a gift that we might call faith.

Somehow I suspect that something akin to this was still operative when Martin Luther King spoke against American policy in Vietnam and said, "I speak not out of anger, but out of love for America and out of the hope that America can change." At this point, how in the world could a black man speak, not out of anger but out of love for America, without something called either the gift of faith or an absurdity that we cannot possibly understand? I think that there must have been some real faith in a man like this and in the millions of others like him who still hold to the possibility that America can change for the better. (On the other hand, one of the things that strikes me as I walk through the ghettos of America, is that there is yet a hope in America's depressed black communities for the coming of a Messiah. Usually this is not a Messiah in any sense that any of us has ever known, and the longing is expressed in words like, "Oh, how could we have lost Malcolm, our Prince? When will we be granted a chance again to have a leader to lead us on the way out?" Such expectations do not express faith in the possibility of change coming from America's own heart, but it is faith nevertheless.) So I am suggesting that the gift of blackness in America is somehow part and parcel of this gift of faith that Paul was speaking about.

* * *

But I see as well in the heart of black America a gift that could only be described, in Paul's concepts, as the capacity to distinguish between the true spirits and the false. For somehow it appears that here in America, if my own experience bears any truth, one of the tremendous gifts that black people have for this society is the gift of reading and telling the American story as it is, not as it is written in most of our textbooks on political science and history. The joys of democracy and the ever-upward-and-onwardness of the American society, have little meaning to the majority of those whose parents were slaves. This is what the late Langston Hughes meant when he said in his marvelous poem, "America, you've never been America to me." This is what Stokely Carmichael meant when, at the Spring Mobilization for Peace, he read American history from the black side. He read it in terms of the burning of the Indians by the Puritans while they gave thanks to God. He read it in terms of the concentration camps that were created for these first families. He read American history in terms of the rape of Mexico. He read American history in the light (or darkness) of the crushing of the Cuban rebellion in 1898. He read American history through the destruction of the Philippine Revolution in the years that followed Cuba. He read American history in terms of the constant North American domination of the Latin nations. He read American history out of the eyes of a black man, eyes that have witnessed thousands of community lynchings and millions of more gradual brutalizations. As a result Carmichael concluded each paragraph by declaring, "We charge genocide."

The gift of distinguishing between that which is true and that which is false about this nation seems to me to be a peculiar gift that is needed very much in the American society today. I think that those of us who are black and who read history, untrammeled by the sweetness and light that we have been taught, may perhaps be able to perform the tremendous task of facing America with the truth, the setting-free truth, the bitter medicinal truth.

I think that blackness contains another gift as well, the

gift of prophecy. The prophet has been described as "one who sees beneath the surface and clearly apprehends the inner hidden trend of events." The prophet in Israel, rather than focusing on the future, often spoke most cogently to the present. Everywhere, he is one who speaks honestly to the people concerning what they say they believe in, and who speaks of what will happen to them if they continue to deny their own vows. I think that many black men in America have been granted the painful position of prophets. For there is surely a need for such a gift in this land today, and we are those who have often been most free to speak with clarity and authority of the unfaithfulness now and the fire *next time.*

But I think that we are beginning to see that the gift of prophecy that the black people have within America is also a gift for the world at large. We should have known this and we should have understood it before. We should have understood when that strange black genius W. E. B. DuBois began speaking at the beginning of this century. We should have heard the judgment concerning present and future when he began saying in 1900 that the problem of the twentieth century would be the problem of the color line, the relation of whites to the darker races of men in Asia, in Africa, in America, and in the islands of the sea. We should have been listening after World War I—that marvelous war that was fought to make the world safe for democracy while more than one hundred Negroes were being lynched each war year. We should have been listening when this same DuBois, one of the few men in America who saw what the war was really about, wrote these words:

> The World War was primarily the jealous and avaricious struggle for the larger share in exploiting darker races. As such it is and must be but the prelude to the armed and indignant protest of these despised and raped people. Today Japan is hammering on the door of justice. China is raising her half-manacled hands to knock next. India is striving for

the freedom to knock. Egypt is sullenly muttering. The Negroes of South and West Africa, of the West Indies and the United States are just awakening to their shameful slavery. Is then this war the end of wars? Can it be the end so long as sits enthroned, even in the souls of those who cry peace, the despising and robbing of darker peoples? If Europe hugs this delusion, then this is not the end of the World War; it is but the beginning.

This was the black gift of prophecy as it was offered to the nation and the world in 1920, but America could not listen. It could not realize that here in the wilderness of this strange and torturous experience known as being black in America, this man was telling the nation what was coming if it did not change its ways. It is the same gift of prophecy that we saw when Martin Luther King spoke about the insane direction of American foreign policy, and we could not put him back into a proscribed box called civil rights. It is the same gift of prophecy that Malcolm X was trying to practice when he spoke about "chickens" of American violence "coming home to roost" at the death of President Kennedy. Perhaps it was one of the closing manifestations of the gift of prophecy that James Baldwin was exercising when he wrote these words:

> We are in the hideous center of a mortal storm which many of us saw coming. Many of us will perish and certainly no one of my generation can hope honorably to survive. And whether or not one agrees with me, I think it is useful to assume that America will not survive this storm either, nor should she. She is responsible for this holocaust at which the living cry out. It is American power which makes death an enviable state for so many millions of people. We are a criminal nation built on a lie and, as the world cannot use us, it will presently find some way of disposing of us. I take this for granted, and the future of this nation, even though it may also be my own, cannot concern me any longer. I am concerned with the living. I am concerned with a new morality and a new creation. I hope I do not sound literary. In any

case, I mean what I say. I really believe that it is possible for human beings to make a place in which we all can live.

Is this the gift of prophecy? Or shall we simply assume that this is another mad, black man not knowing whereof he speaks? The most important thing, though, I think, is that James Baldwin, like many others of these strange, black and tortured prophets, has not spoken out of hatred for America. Rather his words pour out because of a deep concern to find a new and loving way for mankind, and he is convinced that America now stands in the way of this new hope for the world.

* * *

Perhaps words like those of Baldwin and King and Stokely already suggest what I think is the deepest element of the gift of blackness, and that is compassion. For in our pilgrimage through this land there has been much raw material for the building of compassion. We are the rejected ones, the humiliated ones, the spit-upon ones of America. There is much in our experience that may make it possible for us to have some sense of knowing what it means to be among the outcasts of the world, and this knowledge may well be the key to survival in today's world. Before he died, A. J. Muste said that the world was no longer divided between Communists and non-Communists (if it ever was) but the great division in the world is now between those nations who have never known humiliation and those who have known humiliation as a national experience for centuries. We who are black live among the leaders of the arrogant white west, but we've "been 'buked and we've been scorned," and our experience may have been for the world.

There was a strange little bit of dialogue that took place between Walt Whitman and Ralph Waldo Emerson at one point in their lives. Whitman said to Emerson, "Master, I am a man who has perfect faith, but master,

we have not come through centuries, caste, heroism,
fables to halt in this land today." Now in our own time, a
black Whitman has paraphrased those words in a way that
seems to me to be most significant for this gift of compassion. Lerone Bennett transposes Walt Whitman in this
way, "Fellow Americans, we have perfect faith, but,
fellow Americans, we have not come through slavery,
degradation, blood, cotton, roaches, rats to halt in this
land today." Somehow I think these words are saying
that we who have known the rejection of America, the
nation that stands as the paragon of whiteness and "free-
ness" in the world today, are people who must know
what it is that other people are feeling the world around
and we must serve their cause.

What I am suggesting is that those of us who have
known humiliation in this country may well have been
granted the gift of a sense of compassion for the humiliated of the world. And it may be that we shall understand
more clearly than other Americans are able to understand
what it is that the rest of the poor and the dying and
burning world are shouting at America as they try to beat
back our air forces with their rifles and their swords. The
rejected of the world may have spokesmen within the
black heart of American society, spokesmen who perhaps
remember that the loving Father has never disowned any
of his children—not even for being Communists.

This may be our gift, and it is a strange gift to ponder
because we have not usually thought of our position on
such terms. Indeed, I remember James Weldon Johnson,
in his *Autobiography of an Ex-Colored Man,* having his
protagonist say, "I don't want to look at the world with
narrow, constricted Negro eyes; I want to look at it
through human eyes." What he really meant was, "I want
to look at it through white eyes." Now, however, it is
clear that if we simply count up the people in the world,
a man actually sees more when he looks at the world
through nonwhite eyes, partly as a matter of arithmetic,

partly as a matter of history. And the compassion that those eyes may hold, may indeed be a gift worth developing.

I think this is something that needs to be said more fully and more clearly. For it is my own deep conviction that our position as black people in American society gives us a perspective on this society and on this world that makes it possible for us to be free from the deadly narrowness of white American nationalism and self-righteousness. In this kind of trembling world, such freedom is surely a gift, for it is the freedom to care.

It may well be that our position in the American society over the last three hundred and fifty years makes it also possible for us to be free from any need to protect the American system or "the American Way of Life," for we know that a murderous racism is deeply inbedded in that Way. It may be that our experience in America makes it possible for us to extricate ourselves from the strange and mad roles of being military defenders of those outpost investments of American corporate capitalism that are to be found in Africa and Asia and Latin America and Harlem. For as one young man has very rightly asked, "What in the world do black people have to defend when we start talking about investments?" (I think it was Lenin who was so surprised to hear that there were black conservatives in America. He said, "Oh, yes? What do they have to conserve?") And if Negroes stopped volunteering where would our ground level combat forces be?

Surely the blackness of our countenances and the humiliation to which we have been exposed make it sheer madness for us even to consider destroying other people to save American "face." And the other American burnings that are so well recorded in many places, the burnings of black men and women in a thousand Southern village squares ought to make it totally impossible for us, with any kind of conscience or rationality, to engage now in the task of burning other poor people for the American Way of Life.

This isn't simply treason. It is a gift, a gift of God. For I suspect that if we would exercise the gift of our blackness and recognize it and hold it and use it and share it in the way that gifts were meant to be shared, then we might be delivered. We could be delivered to be the brothers to the poor and to the revolutionaries of the world. We would be sprung from the trap of the affluent society to join hands with all those who are seeking to build a new kind of freedom and a new kind of man and a new kind of world, whether they call themselves workers of the kingdom of God or workers for the kingdom of man. I think that our blackness, if properly seen, might make it possible for us to be delivered from the madness of American power, to seek a power that grows neither out of the barrel of a gun nor from the heat of burning jelly. The power of the sons of God.

I think if we properly use our blackness, we shall also be delivered from the falseness of the churches in order to go out and to seek our Lord among his despised and rejected brothers, wherever they may be, whether in Vietnam or Guatemala, Peru or Mozambique, Nashville or New York. This, I suspect, is the deepest meaning of King and Carmichael and Malcolm X. Their lives and words strongly suggest that we who are black live now in the heart of a society that is fighting perhaps its last great series of battles to determine whether it shall be remembered as the most dangerous and cruel society in the world or whether it shall have a chance to be a source of renewed hope for the people of the world.

Therefore we who are black can no longer afford to be parochial. We cannot be American first. (Indeed, no Christian can be that!) Our gift, if it is our gift, like all of God's gifts, is for the world. Therefore, like King and Carmichael, we must now speak and act for the world in the midst of the present American situation. This means that we must be acting and speaking again and again against almost everything that our national leaders identify as the American interest in the world. For whether we like it or not, Americans are now almost consistently against the interests of the poor and the weak and the powerless all over the world. "National Security" for America means universal insecurity upon the earth.

This, I think, is perhaps a part of the new meaning of "Let my people go." Let my people go not from their blackness but from their bondage to American false images and American goals. Let my people go so that they may serve me. This, I think, is what it means. And when we ask, How do we serve Him—or It or whatever he is or wherever he is—then I think the answer comes, and it is this: If he is really dead, it means entering the struggle that he did not complete—the struggle for the children, the burning children, the struggle for the poor, the pressed-down poor, the struggle for the humiliated, the struggle for the weak, the struggle for all those who have paid the debt for the building of a modern society without ever gaining any of its benefits. If he is dead or if he is alive, if he lives somewhere or anywhere or here, serving him means going on in the spirit of that God-intoxicated swinger of a son who was called Jesus Christ. It means that this guy knew what he was talking about when he said that people who are filled with compassionate religious fervor have good news for the poor. They have sight to bring to the blind and they have freedom to work for—for all of the broken victims. This, I think, is the heart of our gift, a sense of what it is that men are trembling about and struggling about and seeking for, so that we are no longer trapped by those foolish clichés about Communism versus "the free world."

The gift of blackness, I think, will open our eyes and clear our head. As I understand it, black men may now be called upon to lead the way to a transformed (and per-

haps humiliated) America, not simply for the sake of
America, but for the sake of the world. Those who are
not black may wish to follow, but I suspect that the
peculiar gift in this task is distinctly ours. For we know
what it means to have suffered for centuries under the
yoke of white Western oppression and at the same time
we are in the heartland of the very yoke. At this moment,
of course, we who are black are obviously uncertain
about what this all means. We need others—as is always
the case with gifts—we need others to help us to perfect
this gift. But it is ours.

So our blackness, in a sense, is like the wings of the
birds. It is a burden when not properly used. But it is a
gift. It is a gift in its highest potential, and it means not
being burdened down. It means free at last. It means
flying. Man, it means like soaring. It means like *real*
soaring.

But of course it's necessary to recognize that our
blackness—as the blues song said—our blackness is also
like a cross. It's the way to both death and life. And
perhaps Baldwin is right. Perhaps we will have to die in
the process of working for those whom America is working against. Perhaps America will have to be crushed if it
continues its ways. But that is not for us to know or to
say. Our gift is the gift of compassion with those who are
crying out from under the alabaster colossus. It is we who
must lead the way and others must follow. Others may
find that they wish to break into the line of seekers after
a new life. Others may find that they wish really to seek
after new ways of living for the world rather than for
individual, narrow American goals. How can this be
done? I am not at this point competent to say. But one
thing certainly can be done and that is that all people
who are not black must certainly encourage every vestige
of black consciousness that they see breaking out among
them. For this is a gift. It seems very clear to me that if

there is nothing else to do, then those who are not black can *rejoice* in the search for black power whenever it seems creative. This is what the members of the body do. They rejoice over the gifts of others; they do not run away in fear: they rejoice.

Perhaps all who really want to glimpse the way might eavesdrop on that marvelous black revolutionary, Frantz Fanon, as he speaks to his nonwhite brothers of the third world in these words from *The Wretched of the Earth:*

> Come then, comrades, it would be well to decide at once to change our ways. [And notice the biblicism of Fanon, of all people!] We must shake off the heavy darkness in which we were plunged and leave it behind. The new day which is already at hand must find us firm, prudent, and resolute. We must leave our dreams and abandon our old beliefs and friendships of the time before life began. Let us waste no time in sterile litanies and nauseating mimicry. Leave this Europe where they are never done talking of man, yet murder men everywhere they find them, at the corner of every one of their own streets and almost every corner of the globe. For centuries they have stifled almost the whole of humanity in the name of a so-called spiritual existence. Look at them today swaying between atomic and spiritual disintegration. Let us decide not to imitate Europe. Let us combine our muscles and our brains in a new direction. Let us try to create the whole man whom Europe has been incapable of bringing to triumphant birth. Two centuries ago a former European colony decided to catch up with Europe. It succeeded so well that the United States of America became a monster in which the taints, the sicknesses, and the inhumanity of Europe have grown to appalling dimensions. It is a question of the third world starting a new history of man. If we wish to live up to our people's expectations we must seek the response elsewhere than in Europe. Moreover, if we wish to reply to the expectations of the people of Europe, it is not good sending them back a reflection, even an ideal reflection of their society. For Europe, for ourselves, and for humanity, comrades, we must turn over a new leaf. We must work out new concepts and try to set afoot a new man.

Those who are not black, but who seek to understand the meaning of the gift of blackness, and those who are black, and seek to understand the nature of their own gifts, must hear Fanon. For Fanon, in the deepest sense, seeks life for all—all who are ready to accept the gift of blackness as it is. And I think that this perhaps is the fullest calling of all those who say, "But what about us, white us?" The calling is most importantly now to understand this point in history, to understand the meaning of what Nat Hentoff calls the "age of black" that is springing up among us. Share where you can, but most of all, rejoice. Rejoice that others have taken the burden that Rudyard Kipling put on your shoulders and follow as you can and as you will. For it must be clear that the gift of blackness will never finally comprehend the gift of healing unless the truth that blackness reveals about our American society and the Western world is clearly acknowledged. The gift of blackness will never comprehend the gift of healing unless this broken, white-oriented, Western-corrupted world seeks for healing and then enters into the healing act, enters in company with the blessed black brothers. For I think the time is now beginning when the first must be last and the last must indeed be first.

If you share that recognition of the meaning of this moment, then you can really rejoice. Then you can hear Stokely and not faint. You can learn from King *and* Fanon. And then you can be men and bear up to what Ronald Fair means when he says, "God, it must be terrible not to be born black in this day and age." If you are men, truly men, and especially if you claim to be men of God, then it will be only terrible, and not deadly, like the terror of the Almighty One. Then you can hear such words and you can say with us, "Tell it like it is, baby Ron, tell it like it is." In other words, *Amen.*

5

Free Who?
ANN BEARD

> *But the act of teaching is usually casual. That is, you can pick up God knows what from God knows who.*

Amiri Baraka (LeRoi Jones)

> *I am the only kind of slave I could stand to be—a bad one. Every day that come and hour that pass that I got sense to make half a step do for a whole; every day that I can pretend sickness 'stead of health; to be stupid 'stead of smart; lazy 'stead of quick—I aims to do it. And the more pain it give Marster and the more it cost him—the more Hannibal can be a man.*

Hannibal in *The Drinking Gourd*
by Lorraine Hansberry

ANN BEARD studied music in Kentucky, New York City, and India. She is presently Children's Project Director, Plymouth Settlement House, Louisville, Kentucky, and a member of the Editorial Board of *Katallagete*.

A Regime that talks most of some value is a regime that consciously or unconsciously denies that value and prevents it from existing.

Jacques Ellul

To be black in America is to live forever on the edge of death at the hands of white people. To come to realize that most of the brothers and sisters who are in this country's jails are there because they did something *right!* and not wrong is to come to realize how close and for *real!* death is for black people.

Liberals are eager to point out and make examples of those blacks who "made it" into the great American system of big business and suburbia and Playtex girdles in spite of the fact that they "just happened to be Negro." And they are even fonder of those they saved from their negritude, their final act of Love Impossible being to send them North to school to have the "best" education and exposure to a culture which would save them from those niggardly "dis 'n dems" and collard greens and fatback and Royal Crown Hair Grease.

Could any liberal believe that our own fathers and mothers and aunts and cousins and friends wanted what was best for us? But that our fathers and uncles and friends had no equations or guidelines for blackness for this had been burned from their consciousness in the Mississippi Delta and Southside Chicago and Berea's Middletown and five-and-dime stores and welfare lines. That when the call went out to send their young, gifted and black North, they could hope only for the best and send us away in spite of their fears, and in spite of all that Aunt Bessie had learned while sweating in Miss Ann's kitchen.

The plan (or "program" as they are so fond of calling their schemes) goes by many names: cultural enrichment programs, high risk, exchange programs. Whites seldom knock at the doors of black families unless they want rent or insurance money, or they come to arrest black people for some crime supposedly committed. They would send a white man to the doors of black families to "look over" the family situation, to see if they were getting the very "best" of black youth. You see, to qualify for their programs, a student had to be long on the road towards success and achievement as defined by white people in their white world. A student had to be National Honor Society material (preferably valedictorian of his or her class), a talented dancer or pianist or artist or speaker or student leader. In other words, a student had to be "it" or super-nigger before he could possibly be considered for such programs.

Then the letters from the national office would start pouring into black homes, and letters from the white families in the great North with whom the black students would be living. And our mothers would sit at the dining room table late into the night trying to make some sense of it all, and to explain it to their black children. There would be an excitement of sorts all around the house and in the neighborhood as our mothers mended old clothes and made a blouse out of scraps which could be worn with two or three skirts; or the little old lady who had taught Sunday School for all of her life would stop by to tell you how proud she was and to slip a dollar into the student's hand; and from somewhere out there in our community would come a new pair of shoes and a silk slip and a scarf. Classmates would stop by to say their goodbyes; and we wondered then if we would ever see them again or what would become of their nice-but-not-super-nigger-type lives.

All of the things would be lovingly packed into old trunks and taken down to the Greyhound Express. And finally, the long ride into the night.

For some of us, it was almost too much: living with white families for two years; being the "only one" in the school; fear of failure and disappointment to those who

loved us back home; countless speeches to the local
Chamber of Commerce and Kiwanis about how much
better it was "up here" than in the South and "No Suh, I
ain't nevuh seen snow and I cain't tap dance, neither";
smiling when there was every reason to cry; being in fact
the only one taking the *real* high risk. But most of all
knowing that they were saying that something was wrong
with the way you had been brought up and your mother's values and your father's job and the food Auntie
cooked and Bobby Blue Bland and Sonny Terry and
Mama shouting in church and the brothers and sisters
gettin' down on Saturday night, and singin' the blues
(unless your white family happened to be super-educated
and thought the blues quaint and nice!) and going home
for vacation and wanting to kiss and hold everyone close
but feeling a kind of stranger and fearing that you would
lapse back into "Negro mannerisms" and have to start
from the beginning and—like our foreparents—having our
black consciousness burned from our beings.

We learned our lessons well, those of us who survived.
We made their kindness worthwhile by graduating with
honors. We learned to carry on very pleasant conversations after Silent Meeting (saying nothing and everything), and to recognize melodic lines from *La Bohème;*
to attend church and sit for *exactly* one hour and never
feel a thing, even though the preacher tried to be hip and
run down a joke or two and the choir sang a glorious
rendition of some obscure Bach cantata. Yes, we proved
beyond a shadow of a doubt that black folks can become
cultured, refined, and polished.

But the lesson we learned with blood and with our
very lives was not supposed to be a part of the curriculum
(or was it?). To have scheduled this class (Liberal Racism
203b, 2:30 MWF) would have stated openly and exactly
who and what they are. If Cynthia and Carol and Denise
and Ada could unearth their now-rotten lips, they would
scream along with all of us:

Integration is a drag. or
"Prepare to meet
(sisters and brothers) the brash and terrible weather;
the pains;
the bruising."

Gwendolyn Brooks

* * *

What does all of this have to do with *her*? You must know of whom I speak, for you read newspapers ("Progress!") and already mass media commentators and newsmen press their black suits and purchase new bow ties to receive their "coveted" Best-Story-of-the-Year awards. They have told you all there is to know. They have told you nothing.

Angela Davis and I (along with others in both our families) participated in such programs; we were victims of love-a-nigger-a-year projects, betcha-I-can-be-more-liberal-than-you mentalities, and unbelievable blindness. We were not strangers to each other. Our paths crossed from Federation Day Nursery to city-wide concerts to summers at Camp Blossom Hill with the Girl Scouts to piano lessons and recitals to the band and National Honor Society at Parker High School to the friends we shared and finally to New York to one such high school program. Our paths have not crossed much since those days in New York, except in the way that all black people's paths must cross. I would see her sometimes at the public library in Birmingham during vacations. She went on to Germany to study philosophy and politics, and I ended up in college where I learned even more about white liberals.

She sits alone in a jail cell now. We are told that when first arrested (kidnaped) in New York City she was placed in a ward for the mentally disturbed where library, recreation, and other privileges were absolutely denied. She ate alone, showered and exercised alone, and her cell was searched three times a day by a guard stationed around the clock. She found roaches in her food, and awoke in terror at night to find rats racing across her body. The intimidations and harassment do not end with her; they are extended cordially to her family. Visiting privileges are taken away for any reason a guard can get by with. Her pregnant sister Fania was shoved and pushed by a matron while she tried to put on her boots to leave the jail. Her mother and father in Birmingham are forever victims of hate at the hands of the local police.

A woman who received the *best* in education at one of New York City's *best* private schools, and who attended the *best* of eastern universities and who studied at one of Germany's *best* universities and who attended one of the West Coast's *best* institutions and graduated from all of them with highest honors now sits alone in a jail spitting roaches out of her coffee. Now we know it all: a nigger is a nigger is a nigger!

* * *

We live in a country where false issues are the word of the day; this is what keeps Americans patriotic and ready to murder the first "gook" who raises his head. It is also the American Way that black people are not immune to sickness and false issues, and that some of us actually believe that Angela Davis is guilty of some crime. To know it all is to know that Angela is not the criminal, but educational institutions, Barbie dolls, political parties, Julie and David, Wall Street, directors of human rights commissions, Sears, TWA, Eastland, Nixon, Reagan, Woolworths.

For fear that the point is missed, let me state: the subject of this article is not Angela Yvonne Davis. The subject is all those white liberals who squeeze their eyes and ball their fists tightly against their reddening cheeks and mouth between clinched teeth, "There is progress! Things have changed. Prog. . . ." The subject is all those who will integration to be a cruel and vicious device to control the niggers who *somehow!* fled the plantation. The subject is all those Great American Institutions (especially the church) which have to this day failed to deal in any positive manner with the racial crisis. Their we-will-hire-anyone-who-is-qualified racism and academic-excellence smokescreen have effectively kept the niggers and undesirables in their places. The subject is all those Christian churches and Christian colleges which have out-caesared Caesar. The subject is White House Prayer Breakfasts. The subject is the For Real! criminals. The subject is slavery and the American way of TV, superhighways, Captain Kangaroo, the little doughboy, commissions, reports, studies, and Mrs. Olson's mountain grown coffee.

And the subject is young, black Jonathan Jackson walking armed into that now famous San Rafael courtroom and announcing to all the world, "Excuse me, gentlemen, I'm taking over now."

PART 2

6

Events and Pseudo-Events:
Letter to a Southern Churchman

THOMAS MERTON

I have publicly stated that I would no longer comment on current events. People ask why. There are many reasons, and I might as well say at once that they are reasons which may possibly be valid for me only, not for others. In any case I did not make this decision for anyone but myself.

First of all, I mistrust an obsession with declarations and pronouncements. While silence can constitute guilt and complicity, once one has taken a stand he is not necessarily obliged to come out with a new answer and a new solution to insoluble problems every third day.

After all, was it not Bonhoeffer himself who said it was

~~~~~~

THOMAS MERTON, until his death in 1968, was a member of the Order of Cistercians of the Strict Observance in the Abbey of Gethsemani, Kentucky. In addition to his autobiography, *Seven Storey Mountain,* his more than thirty books of theology, poetry, devotion, and literary and social criticism include *The New Man, Seeds of Contemplation, The Waters of Siloe, Seeds of Destruction, Raids on the Unspeakable, Conjectures of a Guilty Bystander, Mystics and Zen Masters.*

an "Anglo-Saxon failing" to imagine that the church was supposed to have a ready answer for every social problem?

When one has too many answers, and when one joins a chorus of others chanting the same slogans, there is, it seems to me, a danger that one is trying to evade the loneliness of a conscience that realizes itself to be in an inescapably evil situation. We are all under judgment. None of us is free from contamination. Our choice is not that of being pure and whole at the mere cost of formulating a just and honest opinion. Mere commitment to a decent program of action does not lift the curse. Our real choice is between being like Job, who *knew* he was stricken, and Job's friends, who did not know that they were stricken too—though less obviously than he. (So they had answers!)

If we *know* that we are all under judgment, we will cease to make the obvious wickedness of "the others" a fulcrum for our supposed righteousness to exert itself upon the world. On the contrary, we will be willing to admit that we are "right-wised" not by condemning others according to our law or ethical ideal, but by seeing that the real sinner whom we find abominable and frightening (because he threatens our very life) still has in himself the ground for God's love, the same ground that is in our own sinful and deluded hearts.

To justify ourselves is to justify our sin and to call God a liar.

Second, there is the nature of my own vocation to the monastic, solitary, contemplative life—the vocation of Job! Of course this monastic life does not necessarily imply a total refusal to have anything to do with the world. Such a refusal would, in any case, be illusory. It would deceive no one but the monk himself. It is not possible for anyone, however isolated from the world, to say "I will no longer concern myself with the affairs of the world." We cannot help being implicated. We can be guilty even by default. But the monastic and contemplative life does certainly imply a very special perspective, a viewpoint which others do not share, the viewpoint of one who is not directly engaged in the struggles and controversies of the world. Now it seems to me that if a monk is permitted to be detached from these struggles over particular interests, it is only in order that he may give more thought to the interests of all, to the whole question of the reconciliation of all men with one another in Christ. One is permitted, it seems to me, to stand back from parochial and partisan concerns, if one can thereby hope to get a better view of the whole problem and mystery of man.

A contemplative will, then, concern himself with the same problems as other people, but he will try to get to the spiritual and metaphysical roots of these problems— not by analysis but by simplicity. This of course is no easy task, and I cannot claim that I have discovered anything worth saying. Yet since I have been asked to say something, I will at least hazard a few conjectures. Take them for what they may be worth: they are subjective, they are provisional, they are mere intuitions, they will certainly need to be completed by the thinking of others. If they suggest a few useful perspectives to others, then I am satisfied.

I am more and more impressed by the fact that it is largely futile to get up and make statements about current problems. At the same time, I know that silent acquiescence in evil is also out of the question. I know too that there are times when protest is inescapable, even when it seems as useless as beating your head up against a brick wall. At the same time, when protest simply becomes an act of desperation, it loses its power to communicate anything to anyone who does not share the same feelings of despair.

There is of course no need to comment on the uselessness of false optimism, or to waste any attentions on the sunlit absurdities of those who consistently refuse to face reality. One cannot be a Christian today without having a deeply afflicted conscience. I say it again:—we are all under judgment. And it seems to me that our gestures of repentance, though they may be individually sincere, are collectively hollow and even meaningless. Why?

This is the question that plagues me.

The reason seems to be, to some extent, a deep failure of communication.

* * *

There is a great deal of talk today about the church and the world, about secular Christianity, religionless religion and so on. It seems to me that religionless religion is certainly a result of this failure of communication. (Here I am distinguishing Bonhoeffer's disciples from Bonhoeffer himself.) Seeing that traditional and biblical language simply does not ring any bells in the minds of modern men, the apostles of religionless religion have discarded that language and decided thereby to avoid the problem of communication altogether. Having done so, however, they seem to have also got rid of any recognizable Christian message. To reconcile man with man and not with God is to reconcile no one at all. It is the old problem of the social gospel over again. When the life expectancy of the average secular ideology today is about five years (barring a few notable exceptions that have become orthodoxies, like Marxism and Freudianism) it seems rather irresponsible to identify the gospel with one or the other of them.

Assuming then that the church has something to communicate to the world that the world does not already know, what does this imply? First of all, we must try to clarify the relation of the church to the world. It seems to me false simply to say that the church and the world should be considered as perfectly identified, as indistin-

guishable, and leave it at that. After all, there is still
I John 2:15-16 to be considered.

This judgment of the world as by definition *closed in
upon itself* and therefore *closed to any revelation that
demands to break through its defensive shell* is surely one
of the key ideas of the New Testament. By the Incarna-
tion and Cross Christ does in fact *break through* the
defensive shell not only of sin and passionate attachment,
but of all ethical and religious systems that strive to make
man self-sufficient in his own worldly realm.

The church and the world are related in a dialectic of
identity and nonidentity, yes and no, nearness and dis-
tance. The church is Christ present in the world to
reconcile the world to himself. The world is therefore not
purely and simply Christ. There is a question of acceptance or refusal. If we are dealing with the self-revelation
of a cosmic Christ who is gradually becoming visible in
man, simply *as man*, the decision for this Christ becomes
a kind of poetic commitment to pantheistic vitalism or
something of the sort, not an acceptance of the gospel in
the obedience of faith. In other words "Christ" is then
only a symbol for the world as a closed system. Further,
if Christ is simply manifesting himself in man's history,
whether we do anything about it or not, then there is no
need either of dialogue or of dialectic between the
church and the world. By this dialectic of challenge, faith
and love, word and response, we break out of the closed
system. If we forsake this forward movement toward
eschatological fulfilment, then we plunge into the interminable circling of the world upon itself. No amount of
religious clichés can make this encapsulation a true "freedom."

It seems to me that one of the great obligations of the
Christian is to keep the eyes of his faith clear of such
confusions. And the monk above all has to keep free
from this circling-in-desperation, this closed system,
which is essentially pagan and which implies a hidden

servitude to the elements and the powers of the air in St. Paul's sense (Galatians 4:3, 9). (I readily admit, with Luther, that in practice the monk who makes monasticism a "law" automatically fails in his primal obligation.)

Though there are certainly more ways than one of preserving the freedom of the sons of God, the way to which I was called and which I have chosen is that of the monastic life.

Paul's view of the "elements" and the "powers of the air" was couched in the language of the cosmology of his day. Translated into the language of our own time, I would say these mysterious realities are to be sought where we least expect them, not in what is most remote and mysterious, but in what is most familiar, what is near at hand, what is at our elbow all day long—what speaks or sings in our ear, and practically does our thinking for us. The "powers" and "elements" are precisely what stand between the world and Christ. It is they who stand in the way of reconciliation. It is they who, by influencing all our thinking and behavior in so many unsuspected ways, dispose us to decide *for* the world as *against* Christ, thus making reconciliation impossible.

Clearly, the "powers" and "elements" which in Paul's day dominated men's minds through pagan religion or through religious legalism, today dominate us in the confusion and the ambiguity of the Babel of tongues that we call mass society. Certainly I do not condemn everything in the mass media. But how does one stop to separate the truth from the half-truth, the event from the pseudo-event, reality from the manufactured image? It is in this confusion of images and myths, superstitions and ideologies that the "powers of the air" govern our thinking—even our thinking about religion! Where there is no critical perspective, no detached observation, no time, to ask the pertinent questions, how can one avoid being deluded and confused?

One has to try to keep his head clear of static and

preserve the interior solitude and silence that are essential for independent thought.

A monk loses his reason for existing if he simply submits to all the routines that govern the thinking of everybody else. He loses his reason for existing if he simply substitutes other routines of his own! He is obliged by his vocation to have his *own mind* if not to speak it. He has got to be a free man.

What did the radio say this evening? I don't know.

What was on TV? I have watched TV twice in my life. I am frankly not terribly interested in TV anyway. Certainly I do not pretend that by simply refusing to keep up with the latest news I am therefore unaffected by what goes on, or *free* of it all. Certainly events happen and they affect me as they do other people. It is important for me to know about them too; but I refrain from trying to know them in their fresh condition as "news." When they reach me they have become slightly stale. I eat the same tragedies as others, but in the form of tasteless crusts. The news reaches me in the long run through books and magazines, and no longer as a stimulant. Living without news is like living without cigarettes (another peculiarity of the monastic life). The need for this habitual indulgence quickly disappears. So, when you hear news without the "need" to hear it, it treats you differently. And you treat it differently too.

In this perspective you are perhaps able to distinguish the real happening from the pseudo-event. Nine-tenths of the news, as printed in the papers, is pseudo-news, manufactured event. Some days ten-tenths. The ritual morning trance, in which one scans columns of newsprint, creates a peculiar form of generalized pseudo-attention to a pseudo-reality. This experience is taken *seriously*. It is one's daily immersion in "reality." One's orientation to the rest of the world. One's way of reassuring himself that he has not fallen behind. That he is still there. That he still counts!

My own experience has been that renunciation of this self-hypnosis, of this participation in the unquiet universal trance, is no sacrifice of reality at all. To "fall behind" in this sense is to get out of the big cloud of dust that everybody is kicking up, to breathe, and to see a little more clearly.

When you get a clearer picture you can understand why so many want to stand in the dust cloud, where there is comfort in confusion.

The things that actually happen are sometimes incredibly horrible.

The fog of semi-rational verbiage with which the events are surrounded is also terrible, but in a different way.

And then, beside the few real horrors, there are the countless pseudo-events, the come-on's, the releases, the statements, the surmises, the slanders, the quarrels, the insults and the interminable self-advertising of the image-makers.

We believe that the "news" has a strange metaphysical status outside us: it "happens" by itself. Actually, it is something we fabricate. Those who are poor artisans make only pseudo-events. These are the tired politicians and businessmen, the educators, writers, intellectuals, and, tiredest of all, the churchmen.

Others are better at it: they know how to make real bad news!

Reading the Vulgate I run across the Latin word *simulacrum*, which has implications of a mask-like deceptiveness, of intellectual cheating, of an ideological shell-game. The word *simulacrum*, it seems to me, presents itself as a very suggestive one to describe an advertisement, or an over-inflated political presence, or that face on the TV screen. The word shimmers, grins, cajoles. It is a fine word for something monumentally phony. It occurs for instance in the last line of the First Epistle of John. But there it is usually translated as "idols" . . . "Little children, watch out for the *simulacra!*"—watch out for the national, the regional, the institutional images!

Does it not occur to us that if, in fact, we live in a society which is par excellence that of the *simulacrum*, we are the champion idolaters of all history? No, it does not occur to us, because for us an idol is nothing more than a harmless Greek statue, complete with a figleaf, in the corner of the museum. We have given up worrying about idols—as well as devils. And we are living in the age of science. How could we, the most emancipated of men, be guilty of superstition? Could science itself be our number one superstition?

You see where my rambling has brought me. To this: we are under judgment. And what for? For the primal sin. We are idolaters. We make *simulacra* and we hypnotize ourselves with our skill in creating these mental movies that do not appear to be idols because they are so alive! Because we are idolaters, because we have "exchanged the glory of the immortal God for the semblance of the likeness of mortal man, of birds, of quadrupeds, of reptiles . . . ," we fulfil all the other requirements of those who are under God's wrath, as catalogued by Paul in Romans 1:24-32.

Our idols are by no means dumb and powerless. The sardonic diatribes of the prophets against images of wood and stone do not apply to our images that live, and speak, and smile, and dance, and allure us, and lead us off to kill. Not only are we idolaters, but we are likely to carry out point by point the harlotries of the Apocalypse. And if we do, we will do so innocently, decently, with clean hands, for the blood is always shed somewhere else! The smoke of the victim is always justified by some clean sociological explanation, and of course it is not superstition, because we are by definition the most enlightened people that ever happened.

The things that we do, the things that make our news,

the things that are contemporary, are abominations of superstition, of idolatry, proceeding from minds that are full of myths, distortions, half-truths, prejudices, evasions, illusions, lies: in a word—*simulacra*. Ideas and conceptions that look good but aren't. Ideals that claim to be humane and prove themselves, in their effects, to be callous, cruel, cynical, sometimes even criminal.

We have no trouble at all detecting all this in the ideologies of *other* nations, *other* social groups. That is at least something! But it is not enough. We cannot begin to face our real problems until we admit that these evils are universal. We see them in others because they are in ourselves. Until we admit that we are subject to the same risks and the same follies, the same evils and the same fanaticisms, only in different forms, under different appearances (*simulacra*) we will continue to propose solutions that make our problems insoluble. We will continue to be deadlocked with adversaries who happen to be our own mirror image.

* * *

My thesis is now clear: in my opinion the root of our trouble is that our habits of thought and the drives that proceed from them are basically idolatrous and mythical. We are all the more inclined to idolatry because we imagine that we are of all generations the most enlightened, the most objective, the most scientific, the most progressive, and the most humane. This, in fact, is an "image" of ourselves—an image which is false and is also the object of a cult. We worship ourselves in this image. The nature of our acts is determined in large measure by the demands of our worship. Because we have an image (*simulacrum*) of ourselves as fair, objective, practical, and humane, we actually make it more difficult for ourselves to be what we think we are. Since our "objectivity" for instance is in fact an image of ourselves as "objective," we soon take our objectivity for granted, and instead of checking the facts, we simply manipulate the facts to fit one pious conviction. In other words, instead of taking care to examine the realities of our political or social problems, we simply bring out the idols in solemn procession. "We are the ones who are right, *they* are the ones who are wrong. We are the good guys, *they* are the bad guys. We are honest, *they* are crooks." In this confrontation of images, "objectivity" ceases to be a consistent attention to fact and becomes a devout and blind fidelity to myth. If the adversary is by definition wicked, then objectivity consists simply in refusing to believe that he can possibly be honest in any circumstances whatever. If facts seem to conflict with images, then we feel that we are being tempted by the devil, and we determine that we will be all the more blindly loyal to our images. To debate with the devil would be to yield! Thus in support of realism and objectivity we simply determine beforehand that we will be swayed by no fact whatever that does not accord perfectly with our own preconceived judgment. Objectivity becomes simple dogmatism.

As I say, we can see this mechanism at work in the Communists. We cannot see it in ourselves. True, of course, our dogmatism is not as blatant, as rigid, as bureaucratically dense, as monolithic. It is no less real. That is to say, it is based on *refusals* that are just as categorical and just as absolute.

These refusals are made necessary by a primary commitment to a false image which is the object of superstitious worship. The fact that the image is not made of stone or metal, but of ideas, slogans, and pseudo-events, only makes it all the more dangerous.

* * *

A more complex syndrome is our mythical thinking. I shall call it "justification by snake handling."

Let me say at once that I am not trying to ridicule the good, simple people in the Tennessee mountains or in North Carolina who every once in a while gather in their little churches, work themselves up into a state of exaltation and then pass around a live rattlesnake from hand to hand. There is a kind of rugged starkness about this primitive fundamentalism that calls for a certain respect, and I am reminded that in the novels of Flannery O'Connor due honor was not denied to primitives. The people Flannery O'Connor despised were those whose mental snake handling was more polite and less risky, more sophisticated and adroit, more complacent and much less honest, based on the invocation not of Mark 16:18, but of something at once more sinister, more modern and more obscure.

I take the mountain people as my starting point because in them the cycle is stark and clinically clear. And they are aware of what they are doing.

The rest of us do it without recognizing the analogy.

I do not say we do it every day. Snake handling is reserved for moments of crisis, when we feel ourselves and our ideals called into question. It is our reaction to deep stirring of guilt about ourselves and our image. We handle snakes in order to restore the image to a place of perfect security.

In Christian terms, the mental snake handling is an attempt to evade judgment when our conscience obscurely tells us that we are under judgment. It represents recourse to a daring and ritual act, a magic gesture that is visible and recognized by others, which proves to us that we are right, that the image is right, that our rightness cannot be contested, and whoever contests it is a minion of the devil.

Here is the scenario.

First, a drab, uninteresting, or over-organized, bored

existence. Or at least an obscure feeling that your life is not quite as meaningful as it ought to be. That there is not only something lacking, but probably *everything* lacking. The more obscure and diffuse the feeling, the better. If you are hardly aware of it at all, fine. Most Americans on any day of the week can, if they reflect a little on it, see that they easily meet these qualifications. Even if one has all he needs in material goods, he can still feel as if he lacked *everything!*

Second, you have to connive with a group of other people who feel the same way, at least implicitly. You may perhaps come to an agreement with them in actual discussion together, or you may simply (more often than not) find that you and a lot of other people have all seen the same thing on TV or somewhere and are all reacting to it in the same way. I will not go into bizarre details about snake handling in small fanatical groups of adepts and snake handling on the national level. Let's keep it simple. First you are bored and dissatisfied. Second you find yourself in collusion with others who react as you do to some event.

Implicitly or explicitly you agree on some course of action which is at the same time *symbolic, arbitrary, and dangerous.* These three characteristics are essential. There may be others. But at least the act has to be symbolic. If the symbolism is unconscious, so much the better. The act or event has to be arbitrary, irrational, and in a sense provocative. It must not only be more or less unreasonable, it should, if possible, even openly *defy* reason. Indeed it may be totally irrelevant. If at the same time it is an act which defies morality, public or private, this may enhance its value. But that is not essential. It must at least be basically irrational. If it is completely useless and irrelevant, so much the better. And it must be dangerous, if not physically then at least socially or morally. The event brings one face to face with destruction or grave harm, if not danger to life and limb, then a danger to reputation, to one's social acceptability, one's future.

However, while the event may implicitly defy ostracism or hatred on the part of an out-group, it strengthens the bonds of the in-group, those who have agreed to engage in the symbolic and arbitrary activity together. At this point, we recognize characteristic adolescent behavior, but teen-agers have no monopoly on it, except in so far as we are in fact a teen-age society—a society that likes to play "chicken" not with fast cars, but with ballistic missiles.

The symbolic, irrational, and perilous event must prove something, at least to those who perform it. The thing it attempts to prove must be some basic value in themselves: that they are *alive*, that they are *real*, that they *count*, or (as in the case of the authentic snake handlers) that they are *the Chosen*. In fact, it is a *substitute for divine judgment*. Instead of waiting around in uncertainty, one forces the issue. One does something drastic and "conclusive."

Naturally, not all who enact such events are necessarily believers. One does not have to believe in God—one merely needs to have an "image"! This mental ritual is a component in our contemporary idolatries.

Finally, and this is the point, those who have come together, who have agreed, who have performed the irrational, quasi-initiatory act, who have "proved themselves" thereby, who have stabilized their common image, *are now in a position to judge others*. By creating this situation of challenge, by constructing this "event," they have proved themselves to be "the ones who are right." They have not done this by thinking or reasoning, nor by discussion, dialogue, investigation: they have done it by ritual and initiatory action in which they enjoyed the sense of self-transcendence, of escape from the monotony and the affront of a meaningless existence. And note that it is a cycle that is all the more easily set in motion when existence is in fact more really drab, when the mentality of the participants is more genuinely desperate, when the inner contradictions they seek to escape are all the more inexorable.

Though by its nature this event is arbitrary, unnecessary, and in some sense fabricated, if it is sufficiently drastic it can become far more than a pseudo-event. It can become an act of genuine horror. It can lead to incalculably tragic consequences. If, in handing the rattlesnake around, somebody gets bitten, it is no longer a pseudo-event. Yet nevertheless, in its origin, the event was artificial, fabricated, and indeed uncalled for.

Some examples: on the international level, a paradigm of snake handling and pseudo-event was the Berlin crisis, turned on and off periodically for the sake of effect. It reached its paroxysm in Cuba, and shortly after that Khrushchev's snake-handling days were over.

The big fuss about fallout shelters in this country was another episode of the same kind, and it was our reaction to the Berlin crisis. A purely symbolic and irrational exercise.

The philosophy of escalation, with its mystical degrees and esoteric meanings, is a form of intellectual snake handling. To "think of the unthinkable" is to display one's prowess in handling a cosmic copperhead without dismay. Since the copperhead is only abstract at the time the feat is not uncomfortable. But in this area myths can suddenly and without warning turn into unpleasant realities. In point of fact, our snake handling in Southeast Asia is not abstract—but, as I said before, I am not commenting on events.

On another level, we all participate in one way or another in this national or international snake handling when we get into the act in some more or less dramatic way. A lot of our protests and demonstrations, even when they are perfectly valid and reasonable in themselves, take the form of political snake handling. This, I submit, robs them of their real value, because it isolates our action and protest in a closed realm of images and idols which mean one thing to us and another to our adversaries. *We no longer communicate. We abandon communication in order to celebrate our own favorite group-myths in a ritual pseudo-event.* "News" is largely made up of this liturgy of pseudo-events and irrelevant witness. Let us realize that "ideals" and "purity of heart" may easily cover a snake-handling approach to political reality.

Everywhere, from extreme right to extreme left, we find people in our society who become "sanctified," set apart, chosen, sealed off in a ritual game of some sort by reason of events enacted in honor of images. They move step by step, taking the nation with them, into realms of commitment and of absurdity, areas where, by virtue of the fact that one has agreed to face some very select irrationality, *one is quarantined from the ordinary world of right and wrong.*

The man who has agreed with his peers in the enactment of a symbolic, dangerous, and arbitrary event has thereby put himself and them beyond good and evil. They have all entered together into the realm of the gods, and in that realm they find that their action has had amazing consequences: it changes the whole meaning of truth and falsity, it imposes on life an entirely new logic: one must follow on from one irrationality to the next in a demonic consistency dictated by machines.

But here, of course, I am speaking of mental snake handling only at the highest and most mystical echelons of the technological elite. Down on our pedestrian level there is no such mystical security, no such permanent election. We are not initiated into a whole new kingdom of sacred irresponsibilities. We have to repeat some crude fanatical stunt again and again because it never quite takes. However, we have the privilege of remotely participating in the snake-handling exploits of the high priests of policy and strategy.

On this liturgy of pseudo-events the survival of the human race—or at least its sanity and dignity—are now made to depend.

Our salvation, on the contrary, cannot be sought in this realm of images and idols, of fabricated events and unclear meanings.

* * *

After all this rambling and conjecturing, it is time to draw a few conclusions. Should the church turn to the world of modern man and identify with him completely? In all his legitimate aspirations, in all his authentic human hopes and aspirations, obviously it must. If not it betrays him and betrays the gospel. "In so far as you did it to one of the least of these my brothers, you did it unto me" (Matthew 25:40). But the church betrays herself and modern man if she simply identifies with his superstitions, his image-making, his political snake handling and his idolatries of nation, party, class, and race.

The church has an obligation *not* to join in the incantation of political slogans and in the concoction of pseudo-events, *but to cut clear through the deviousness and ambiguity of both slogans and events by her simplicity and her love.*

"To be simple," says Bonhoeffer, "is to fix one's eye solely on the simple truth of God at a time when all concepts are being confused, distorted and turned upside-down. It is to be single-hearted and not a man of two souls. . . . *Not fettered by principles but bound by love for God.* The [simple man] has been set free from the problems and conflicts of ethical decision."

It is unfortunately true that the church has to repent of remaining enclosed in parochial concerns, and turn to the outside world. To turn to the world is to recognize our mission and service to man and man's world. We are not in the world for ourselves, for our own spiritual advantage, but for Christ and for the world. We have a mission to reconcile the world with Christ. How can we do this if we do not "turn to the world"? At the same time, in turning to our fellow man and loving him, we will ourselves be reconciled with Christ. What other point has there ever been in preaching the gospel? Unfortunately the simple business of "making converts" has sometimes obscured all deep understanding of what this turning to the world really means as *event*.

The church is indeed concerned with news: the Good News. The church is concerned with real events: saving events, the encounter of man and Christ in the reconciliation of man with man. In a sense, there is no other kind of event that matters and there is no other news that matters. To abandon this news, and become implicated in the manufacturing of pseudo-events in order to create an "image" that will then attract converts. . . . This is an affront to the world and to Christ. Can it be entirely avoided? I do not know, but one thing must be said about it now: *it has ceased to have any meaning whatever to modern man.*

If *image* means *idol*—and it does—then the church too can unfortunately make an idol of itself, or identify itself too closely with other idols: nation, region, race, political theory.

Obviously the church is present in history and is responsible to man in his historical predicament. But let us not take too superficial and too distorted a view of history. Our oversensitive awareness of ourselves as responsible for "making history" is a grotesque illusion, and it leads us into the morass of pseudo-events. Those who are obsessed with "making history" are responsible for the banality of the bad news which comes more and more to constitute our "history." The church that takes all this too literally and too seriously needs to go back

and read the New Testament, not omitting the Book of
Revelation.

The genuine saving event, the encounter of man with
Christ in his encounter of love and reconciliation with his
fellow man, is generally *not newsworthy*. Not because
there is an ingrained malice in journalists but because
such events are not sufficiently visible. In trying to make
them newsworthy, or visible, in trying to put them on
TV, we often make them altogether incredible—or else
reduce them to the common level of banality at which
they can no longer be distinguished from pseudo-events.

Finally, no matter how you doctor it, *the pseudo-event
cannot be turned into a saving and reconciling event.*
Whether it is a display of political snake handling, or
some other demonstration of man's intent to justify his
existence by seeing himself in the morning paper, no
matter how noble and how Christian the intention may
be, no man is ever going to come to the truth through
pseudo-events, or be reconciled with his fellow man as a
result of pseudo-events. On the contrary, by its very
nature the pseudo-event arouses anxiety, suspicion, fear
of deception, and a full awareness of the inherent weakness of the position which it is supposed to justify.

The great question then is, How do we communicate
with the modern world? If in fact communication has
been reduced to pseudo-communication, to the celebra-
tion of pseudo-events and of incompatible myth-systems,
how are we to avoid falling into this predicament? How
are we to avoid the common obsession with pseudo-
events in order to construct what seems to us to be a
credible idol?

It is a nasty question, but it needs to be considered, for
in it is contained the mystery of the evil of our time.

I do not have an answer to the question, but I suspect
the root of it is this: if we love our own ideology and our
own opinion instead of loving our brother, we will seek

only to glorify our ideas and our institutions and by that fact we will make real communication impossible.

I think Bonhoeffer was absolutely right when he said our real task is to bear in ourselves the fury of the world against Christ in order to reconcile the world with Christ —(a statement that does not accord with the superficial worldliness of some of Bonhoeffer's disciples). But let us take care that the fury of the world is not merely directed against our own ethical or political ideals, worse still our *image* of ourselves incarnated in our particular mode of symbolic protest.

When I began this letter I did not promise an answer, I only promised a question. Our own lifetime will not suffice to bring us close to the answer. But the root of the answer is the love of Christ and the ground is the sinful heart of sinful man as he really is—as we really are, you, and I, and our disconcerting neighbor.

7

Footwashing or the New Hermeneutic?

WILL D. CAMPBELL

What will the racial situation be in the churches of the South when the Yankees have all gone home? They said they came because we had done so little. We may question the conjunction, but not the assertion on either side of it. They *did* come. And we *had* done so little.

How short a time ago it was that they came! We had heard the talk of the long, hot summer. Then they came. Several of them we killed. Then the rest went away. At least most of them went away, though none to our knowledge went away because we killed several of them. Most stayed longer because of that.

How short a time ago it was that the Ivy League doctors—mostly the teaching, preaching doctors, but a few of the doctoring doctors—were here. There were the calls to take them bail or to visit them. Was it Birming-

WILL D. CAMPBELL is Director of the Committee of Southern Churchmen and publisher of *Katallagete.* He is the author of *Race and the Renewal of the Church* and, with James Y. Holloway, editor of *Up to Our Steeples in Politics.*

ham, Montgomery, Albany, or Jackson? Was it freedom
ride, voter registration, or sit-in? Anyway, they were here
and we were glad, and now they are gone. Sometimes one
hears that they are a part of the Clergy Concerned with
the War in Vietnam—a worthy cause, God knows, but
how fickle they are, our Yankee brothers.

They came to be our conscience because we let expec-
tant citizens be shot down in the streets and little girls be
slaughtered at their prayers. But conscience is not a thing
of the moment. It is a thing of generations. It could not
be remade in one summer or two.

There was the Mississippi Project, the FDP, and COFO,
baptized in Oxford, Ohio, and confirmed somewhere
between there and Neshoba County, where three at once
were buried in the red clay of a government dam.

Surely such an offspring would last for a long time.
But it didn't. It is true that a law was passed, and then
another; and more are proposed after Wallace showed us
once more what we should have known all along about
the South, and while senators tell us what we should have
known about the North—"Any further legislation is clearly unconstitutional on its face." (Southern rednecks are
one thing. Northern rentals and bossings are another.)

Meanwhile there were more than twenty race-related
murders in the South in a one-year period following the
Civil Rights Act of 1964, making that the bloodiest since
the Movement began.

And yet they have all gone away. At least almost all of
them. And surely their dream is gone—the dream that the
Mississippi Project, the FDP, and COFO would arouse
that latent goodness supposed to be in all men, Southern
and Federal, and that we would rise up to stay the evil
passion of racism. That dream is gone. From that we have
awakened. The dream of a degree of justice remains, and
thank God. That is an important dream. But the dream of
reconciliation based on the coming of the Yankees is
gone. If one does not believe it, then let him go to a

tavern in Tennessee and hear the manager say, following the visit of a thirsty black man, "Yes, we have to serve them, but we break every glass they drink out of. There's no law against that." That may be justice, but it is not reconciliation. Or let him go into a truck stop with a black friend and watch the waitress stroll casually to the jukebox. Hear her dime produce the words, sung to well-composed and equally well-played music:

> *Move them niggers north.*
> *Move them niggers north.*
> *If they don't like our Southern ways,*
> *Move them niggers north.*

There is no law against playing the jukebox. Not yet. To say nothing about the dangers of having one.

* * *

Where is the reconciliation? In fact, where is the justice? Is there really any justice in a hamburger? Or does the jukebox negate even the hamburger, for who could hold it down? Anyway, most of them are gone. SNCC—though not really North—remained, but after they declared their intention of becoming all black, their dream of "beloved community" became a spasm—at least for white churchly folk. And the Delta Ministry remains in name, but days after their Poor People's Conference sought to take over the Greenville Air Base, a faction of that Conference sought to take over the leased property of the Delta Ministry *at gunpoint!* Folks don't like such ingrates as that, especially if the enthusiasm and financial support from back home are on the wane. The Freedman's Bureau, one of the more promising programs to come South following the Civil War, folded after six years. It did so because the lack of financial support discouraged its advocates to the point of giving up. A

very similar thing is happening now, and we may anticipate an early departure of those whom some saw as
hostile invaders and others regarded as our last hope. Who
then will remain?

We will. We who were born here, who partly created
and partly fell heir to what we have come to call "the
race problem." Black and white, Christian, Jew, and
pagan, we remain. And we will remain. If anyone does.

And what hope is there among *us*? There are indigenous black groups and interracial organizations to
which we can still look for help. Help, but not Messiah.
Even the all-black policy of many may be at once judgment and long-range hope. Those individuals now involved, however, may see the promised land of true
reconciliation (which they verbally reject but still yearn
to see) only from an isolated mountain, standing there
alone, with neither leader nor follower. Though wrought
with so many internal problems that the sophisticated
white liberal sees little hope, they may yet be the tailor
for the sackcloth and ashes which we continue to shun,
but which remains the only acceptable garment for an
audience with the Almighty.

* * *

But what hope is there among us, within us, the
church? If by that one means the institution, after forty
years within it we sadly conclude—*none!* For there is
little to indicate that we are any different today from
what we were in 1954, in 1964, and in 1969. If we see
the all-black policy of SNCC as the hardened heart
which God uses as his judgment upon a segment, then we,
the churches, may be the hardened heart which he uses as
judgment upon us all.

If we are to be honest, we must admit that at the
congregational level the white church in the South has
not yet had the slightest involvement in the racial crisis.
A few pastors have joined an occasional march. A few

more have signed statements. But the fact is that most of these do not march or sign statements or serve as pastors any longer; their flocks not only did not follow them to street and parchment, but they did not tolerate the controversy resulting from their shepherds' strange behavior. If the drought of direct action has been acute during the past few years, the drought of preaching is chronic. Embarrassed with the "Bible Belt" label that the Fundamentalists have caused us to bear, most of us theological sophisticates have shied away from a doctrine of man rooted deeply in Scripture, the doctrine which rejects race as a category. Instead, we have turned to the more scientific and neutral documentation for such preaching as we have done on the subject. Our flocks have rejected social analysis and political meddling as none of the preacher's business—as they should have done (though their reasons were wrong)—so that our congregations have been left to flounder in the mire of religion, the curse of man which Christ sought to dispel, but which continues to dominate us in such proportion as to approach anti-Christ.

But let us not speak now of the churches. Let us speak now of churchmen. Let us confess that we failed to admit the frailty of institutions from the beginning. Had we done so, we would not now sink into despair about the inadequacies of the institutional church. And it is no good to talk now of "para-church." Whatever ways for witness we may find as Christians will be the witness of *church*, or it will not be witness at all.

And there are at least two embarrassments which we must overcome. The first is the embarrassment of biblicism. The second is the embarrassment of the sects. They may well be treated together.

* * *

Partly because we rejected Fundamentalism as adolescents (and the seminaries gave us a sounder basis of criticism to sustain the rejection), and partly because we saw the evils of institutionalized biblical literalism, we turned away from seeking answers in the Scriptures. While the religious racists indoctrinated the South with biblical distortions, we theologically trained sophisticates retreated to . . . the New Hermeneutic! No one will deny that a hook and ladder is better equipment for fighting a fire than a garden hose. But the house is on fire. There is no time to send to Detroit for hooks and ladders. There is no time to await scholarly research—unless, of course, we will enjoy the Stoic satisfaction of consoling ourselves, as observers, that the fire might have been put out long after the embers are dead.

The point is a simple one. Everything else has failed. There has been no reconciliation. There has been precious little social change. Remember how we used to scoff at the "moderates" when they said, "What they are doing will set race relations back fifty years!" We should still be dubious of this and all other clichés. But it is more and more obvious that the social changes have not seen a corresponding change in the basic human relationships of one man to another—black to white and white to black. Such interpersonal relationships are not considered important by those who see the change of the structures as our greatest hope. But structures are persons, groups of persons, who lean in the same direction at a given point in history, just as presidents, senators, and Supreme Court justices read the morning paper to learn the direction in which their followers are leaning.

And although it is denied by both groups, white liberals are cooling off at a rapid pace, and a considerable element of the civil rights movement is moving pell-mell into the yawning lap of Black Nationalism. Thousands who referred to the justice, rightness, and necessity of the Selma march of 1965 referred to the "Sweet Willie Wine" 1969 Memphis to Little Rock march as a civil rights williwaw without meaning or purpose. Yet, we fail to see the difference if either had to do with injustice, for there was as much injustice on the road from Memphis to Little Rock in 1969 as there was from Selma to Montgomery in 1965.

And the denominational commissions on race are roughly back where they were four years ago—passing resolutions deploring this or that, and urging individual church members to wire the President.

* * *

Great God Almighty!

What does, what could, what will, the President of the United States ever have to do with the witness of the church? And when will we quit seeing him as our spiritual head?

Why are we back where we were after those exciting years of more or less active participation in the Movement? The answer again is simple. More and more white folks are seeing that the Movement is not about coffee and hamburgers, or black and white together, but rather is about a more equitable distribution of the goods and opportunities that whites have simply because they are white. And more and more Movement leaders don't want whites involved because they don't, they can't, trust them. In 1965 all the established church groups were issuing nationwide appeals for marchers to go to Selma. There were no such appeals in 1966 for participation in the Mississippi marches. There were some tactical reasons offered, but the real, the big reason was that those appeals in 1965 resulted in too many white folks who marched and dominated the march. If there is one prophetic role the National Council's commissions and departments of Christian social relations can play now, it is to tell white Christians the truth, however painful and unpopular it might be: *stay home!* Anyone who was surprised with the Black Power development must never have read the Bible or history, for the development began when the first slave ship departed the shores of Africa.

* * *

But enough of saying things are worse. Actually things are not worse for everyone. We are not saying that. Things are better for a fairly large number of blacks. Things are also better for a fairly large number of whites, for *they* are better off, economically. The recent civil rights legislation and the Office of Economic Opportunity programs have had some effect within the culture. Not much, but some.

When we speak of things being worse, we are talking of institutionalized Christianity being worse. It is worse simply because it is not better. It is not better because it remained where it was twenty, ten, two years ago, protective of its own, self-loving and largely self-worshiping, while the world whirled by.

So where do we turn? One thing that all other institutions have learned from the civil rights movement is that the very structures which they assumed to be sacred were not sacred after all. Restaurant owners learned that there was nothing as sacred about property rights as they had thought. School boards are learning that there is nothing as sacred about neighborhood schools as they had thought. ("If you can go to the moon, you can bus our children across town.") Only the churches continue to insist that their structures are sacred. As long as they are sacred, they will be stagnant and sterile. A sacred tool is one not to be used but to be fondled and polished. Howard Moody says the church is an instrument of God literally to be used up in his service, a service to those not even within it. There is little evidence at this point in God's economy that the church is about to go out of business through such usefulness.

But there has been a segment of the church whose

idols have been less secure than mainline white Protestantism. These have been what we call the fringe churches, the sects. And what do they do that others don't? Well, they wash one another's feet, they shout, they sing jazzed-up songs to guitar music, they handle snakes. They do all sorts of things. But *what* they do is not so important for our concern as the zeal with which they do it. They do it with zeal because they really believe it. And since they really believe in what they do, the tools they employ are not so important for them. A silver basin is fine for washing feet, but a galvanized foot tub is just as good. An air-conditioned brick building is all right for handling snakes, but a brush arbor is just as good. Acoustical tile would be dandy for shouting, but an unpainted frame ceiling is just as good.

But aside from those things they do, a case can be made that they were more faithful in the racial crisis all along than the established church.

Consider Horace Germany. Horace, a white man, had lived all his life in rural Neshoba County, Mississippi. He made his living by farming. He was also a Church of God preacher. Ten years ago we saw him for the first time. He was lying on his side, his back purple and sore from a beating he had just received from his neighbors. He told this story only after a letter of introduction was shown to him, written by a Church of God preacher in another state.

He had wanted to build a school for Church of God young people who had been called to preach. He would teach them tentmaking, of whatever variety they chose. They would study the Bible, and they would do it without regard to race, for he said he believed that the gospel was a "universal gospel to all men, as given by Christ in the Great Commission. All men are made one in Jesus Christ."

To reach his school, it was necessary to drive down a country dirt road which came very near the scene where some years later three civil rights workers were to be murdered and buried. About three miles down that recently graded, winding and sloping dirt road, hardly wide enough for two cars to pass, there was an open gate at the top of the slope. Through the wooded area there was a clearing and a large pond, the kind the US Department of Agriculture builds for farmers to water cattle. Beside the pond was a long shed with lumber stacked almost to the tin roof. Outside the shed were more lumber and concrete blocks, some with black mildew and spider webs, indicating that this building material had been accumulated over an extended period of time. In the center of the clearing there was the foundation and part of the first story of a large building. This was the beginning of the school.

And it was the beginning of Horace Germany's troubles. A week earlier a large crowd—including, no doubt, some blood cousins as well as Christian brothers of ours—had gathered at one of the mainline churches in the area. Some two hundred could be accommodated inside, and another estimated five hundred formed a sea of solemn faces on the dry, dusty lawn and pressed as closely as possible to open doors and windows in order not to miss the important proceedings inside.

There were the customary prayers that must precede any event in church, but a minimum of preliminaries. They were there to discuss the school construction down the road. A resolution was presented, discussed, and then adopted with a voice vote consisting of shouts—shouts not generally heard in the services of that denomination. The resolution asserted that the school was seeking to destroy harmony between the white and colored races of the area. "The college is purportedly a Christian educational institution," the resolution stated, but "we are convinced that the purpose of this college is to promote, foster, and encourage violence and to disrupt goodwill between the races."

Following the meeting at the church a committee of two hundred waited upon Brother Germany and delivered this message: "Preacher, this is it! We mean, this is it! You get your family and them imported niggers (he already had several students) away from here within forty-eight hours, or we will not be responsible for what happens." Horace reported wryly that "liquor and tobacco smelled strongly, and some of them talked rough."

The newsletter which they mailed regularly to friends and supporters reported the events that followed:

> On Friday, August 26, Pres. Germany, Vice Pres. Burns, and three of our brethren drove into Union where we had bought part of a school building. They were loading material onto the truck when a mob of five or six carloads came, drove the Colored brethren away at the threat of their lives, and set into beating Bro. Germany in a most unmerciful manner with blackjacks, fists, clubs, and while he was on the ground they would kick him. It was one of the most outrageous things that has happened since the establishment of any form of law and order in the United States, especially in connection with the activity of the Church. At this writing Bro. Germany is still in the hospital.

He talked sadly of his shattered dream. We asked him what he planned to do. He said that he wasn't afraid. "Jesus died for me, and I will die for him. I could finish the school all right. People from all over the country have said they would bring their trailers and tents and stand guard until the school is finished. But all I would prove is that I am not afraid. I could build the buildings, but it wouldn't be a school. There would be no students. A school is not a school without students."

"And what will you do with what you have built?"

He turned slowly away and gazed steadily at the wall. A plaster of paris plaque, looking at once like those won at county fair carnivals and the kind made by children at vacation Bible schools, hung on the wall with the inscription: "In all thy ways acknowledge him, and he will direct thy path."

"Yesterday morning one of the biggest bootleggers in the county sent word that he wanted to buy the property. I know what he wants with it. He wants to make a dance hall out of my school and sell whiskey."

"And will you sell it to him?"

"Yes," he said. "Yes, I'm going to sell it to him. I told these people that if they won't let God do his work in this county, the Devil will sure move in and do his. There's a lot more to this race problem than just segregation."

* * *

And how right he was. Maybe those who killed Mickey and James and Andy in Neshoba County that night got the courage to do it from a bottle from what began as the Bay Ridge Christian College.

There were numerous others from the sects who were both prophetic and courageous in the racial crisis. There was James Willis Vaughn, a tall, raw-boned preacher from one of the most rigidly Fundamentalistic sects, who preached a revival at Bethlehem Temple in Jackson, Mississippi, and because the host under whose roof he slept was black, he was fined five hundred dollars, and he and his wife spent sixty days in jail.

But the point for us is not who they were and what they did, but what *we* can learn from *them*.

We are not suggesting that we turn seminaries into training centers for learning to handle copperheads and wash one another's feet—though if Aubrey Norvel would wash James Meredith's feet, and Meredith would let him do it, we would be for setting Norvel free.

The real point is that the idols of the sects are not as secure as those of the established church. When the Yankees have all gone home, this may be the hope for renewal if we in the establishment can learn to think sect!

And what does "think sect" mean? It means brush arbors and communion on a kitchen table. It means preaching on street corners and baptizing in a mill pond or out of a coffee cup. It means Clarence Jordan buried in a pine box in south Georgia. It means Tom Merton's Masses at his hermitage in Nelson County, Kentucky, and the Berrigans' Masses and baptisms in living rooms and in the corners of Protestant chapels and in the streets.

It means poverty. The institutional church stands to-day exactly where the rich young ruler stood in Matthew 19 (and it stands before the same Lord). He was rich, he was powerful, he was good. The church is rich. It is powerful. And it is good. No one ever calls it bad. It is high on the list of agencies to do good in the community when the need arises. The United Fund, the Boy Scouts, the Lions International, the Red Cross, the church—each will accept its quota of responsibility. Yet the reply of our Lord was to get rid of all that and then come and be a disciple.

Think sect means carrying a cyanide capsule in your navel against the day the enemy is so strong against you that the only way you can preserve that with which you have been entrusted is to kill yourself. The enemy is now that strong against us. The enemy has made us rich, powerful and good, knowing that when there was a racial crisis or a Vietnam war, the best we would risk would be debates and resolutions and petitions. The cyanide capsule tucked in our navel is Matthew 19. Let us now swallow it with a joyful gulp. Sell the steeple, the organs, the gold cups, the silver hats, the mahogany pews and the valuable downtown property and give the money away. Give it to BEDC, to the Fentress Low Income People (FLIP), to the poor in the Ku Klux Klan, or simply to those of the poor who happen to be nigh. Don't ask if they are from the deserving or the undeserving poor. Just give it away.

And think sect. Then shout Hallelujah! Then sing the psalms. Then *follow!* But above all, remember that with that one act, Jesus did not offer to the rich young ruler the end of discipleship. That act only qualified him to approach the starting line of discipleship.

Think sect.

8

An Open Letter to Billy Graham

WILL D. CAMPBELL
JAMES Y. HOLLOWAY

There is no prophetic vocation in asserting the failure of institutions to meet the crises of the twentieth century. There is no merit in proclaiming that institutions are twined together with these very crises.

For years we have argued against our liberal brothers that governments, churches, industries, schools, magazines, journals, hospitals, businesses, the media, colleges, unions, service clubs, each in its own way has rationalized the twentieth century into pseudo-events of cold war, secularism, democracy, socialism, Communism, overkill, pollution. We are kept from the crises that might cleanse as they destroy, redeem as they judge. The chief function of institutions today is to perpetuate themselves by perpetuating myths. Illusion is reality! Form is substance! Current "events" are crises! Style is performance! Doing is being! "Direct" action the only action.

Institutions institute inhumanity. They can only dehumanize the relationship between those they were instituted to serve. So blacks, browns, reds, and rednecks in America—not scholars and scientists—retain the passion to understand and describe the dehumanizing effect of two centuries of "the American experiment" on both land and people. Students—not teachers—experience the institution of education as one with the inhumanity of the twentieth century. The young—not the critics of culture—grasp and thus suffer the deceits, definitions and chicanery of cultures that exist to deny freedom to be human: to be with the other in freedom. The alienated Christian—not the mainliner—suffers the blasphemies done Christ by the toadings of Christian leaders to the current kings of Israel and Judah.

Nothing is novel about the foregoing assertions. Radicals and reactionaries alike assert that it has "always been that way with institutions!" That "by definition" an institution can only rationalize and systematize the relationships between men, and thereby dehumanize what previously was a more humane relationship. No doubt they are right. But that is not our point. Our point concerns today, and us: our point is that because of the linking of politics and technique, what defines the technological era is the capacity of its institutions to complete the dehumanizing of mankind. Institutions in previous eras sought to do the same thing but failed simply because they lacked the strength which institutions today have.

So what we see as critical is not the fact of institutional failure, but the *character* of it. That—and the Christian's role in that failure. Law and politics serve not the citizen, but the legal and political machinery: the bureaucracies and enterprises of the military, industrial, technological, scientific, welfare, governmental complex. What can "reforms" net, what do "elections" mean, when the irresistible direction of government is the institution of inhumanity? Invariably, something like the fate of the various "Commissions" to study violence, political assassination, etc., etc., or something like the elections of 1964 or 1968, or the reforms of the Mine Health and Safety Act of 1969. No easing of the misery of those ground into the waste heaps of our technological society, but mythologizing and assuaging the uneasy conscience of the affluent, and extending bureaucratic exploitation to even more phases of life.

* * *

For example, medicine serves not so much the sufferer as the practitioner and the industries of medicine. The media attend to interests of the owners and manipulate readers and viewers toward those interests. Education is about money, buildings, offices, the stock market, secretaries, private offices, tenured and ambitious professors, social engineers, architects, deans, committees, and presidents. Theology and ethics obey the ideological commitments of the theologians and ethicists. And when interests coincide—as in the twentieth century they do around war and around the efforts to purge from society what cannot be assimilated into it (another form of "war")—politics, government, college, labor, churches, seminaries, foundations, Army, FBI, and charitable organizations are indistinguishable from one another by what they "do" to serve these interests. We are not talking about a "conspiracy" among the leaders of these or other institutions, but of something more serious—of the fact that in our day, institutions move in only one direction, and their principal energies digest, assimilate, rationalize, dehumanize any and all "reform." What does it mean, therefore, to "pray" to get the "good" men "in control" of institutions which, in the words of Hosea, make all men "detestable like the thing they love"?

And do not think we are saying that no "good" can come within institutions. We know that "there is no limit to God's grace!" But we are saying that the "good" that occurs is incidental to, a by-product of, the service institutions are "instituted" to render. Thus some quality of justice with order is found, here and there, in all modern governments, but this is incidental to the move toward totalitarianism that governments without exception follow in the twentieth century, and forms of government, good intentions, even prayer and Christian piety have nothing to do with it. Some "education" takes place in institutions of education, but it is a by-product and not the result of the direction of institutional education today, which functions to adjust youth to the technological order. True, some are "led to *Christ*" in the instituted church today, but it is done against the stream of five-point grading programs, censors hovering over "Sunday school" literature or "evangelistic crusades" and "Explos" planned and executed more like the Pentagon than St. Paul.

* * *

Where is the "gospel" in all this? If Jesus' account of why the Samaritan is "good" means anything, it means that those who call him Lord! Lord! are themselves called only to serve *men*, not offices, committees, colleges, sacraments, complexes, faculties, agencies. Maybe one works there. Maybe not. But it seems clear to us Jesus is saying that to follow him one must be known by who he *is*, not by what institution he belongs to. Indeed, he serves the institution by refusing to be subservient to it.

There is no Christian social strategy. And that means that there is no Christian "vocation" the way our bourgeois civilization tried to enforce—having to do with "making a living." These are simple points in our sophisticated and complicated culture, but they have the power to make radical—in Jesus' sense—who individuals *are*.

To say it another way, who spread all those lies about Jesus? Who said that we can serve him only through the agency of institution and ordination, given their authority not by Christ but by Caesar? Who said that we serve only where the churches, their theologians, the Supreme Court and the President of the United States in their desperation, tell us to serve? Who spread the lie about Jesus that "the church" is a thing, a name, a physical setting: consecrated water, pews, altar cloths, smoke, budgets, computers, bricks, grape juice, bowling alleys, key cards, ordained men (only men), air conditioning, Sunday school boards, parking lots, and the American Association of Theological Schools? Who spread such a lie that denies what the church of Jesus is about, and so lied about the church being a relationship, say, like the one between the man in the ditch and the Samaritan? Or between Jesus and Peter, whose confession that Jesus is Lord is the rock upon which *Jesus* says *he* builds *his* church? Or, a relationship which Jesus empowers and authorizes, between man and God and man and man, like unto the relationship between Jesus and God, and Jesus and man? Who spread the lies? Not the New Testament. Not the Old—we have Jesus' word on that.

* * *

What we are talking about is not the fact, but the *character* of the failure of institutions. That character suggests to us something about the way the Christian relates himself to institutions. But most important is what Jesus himself says about himself, and us, about these matters. And that suggests to us that Christians in fear and trembling must examine their relationships to institutions. Right now. Beginning with the ones in which we so long took hope.

We are not talking about "blowing up" institutions any more than we are talking about putting the axe to the computer—actions which relate us to institutions (and to computers) more securely than the most dedicated president (or technician). Rather, we suggest as a minimum and starting point that the real "copouts" today may be those who worship in zeal and dedication "their" institutions (and "their" place in them), who may even on scheduled occasion try to reform them, all the while cursing as "copouts" those who see such carryings-on as exercises in idolatry as well as futility.

Who cops out? The reformer and activist who is hostile and intolerant of those who fail to accept *his* definition of "copout," "reform," and "action"? Or those who try to call attention to the quality of institutional failure? Who cops out? Those who seek to serve their Lord by reforming the unreformable? Or those who seek to serve their Lord by being a neighbor to them who are nigh, even those who like themselves are part of institutions?

Who cops out? The men whose service to their institutions found them so committed elsewhere that they were unable to serve the man their very commitments had helped to throw in the ditch? Or the Samaritan? Who cops out? The men who rejected the story of the Samaritan as individualistic, lacking in social sensitivity, and undermining the positive programs for good the institutions were following? Or the man who told the story of the Samaritan and lived it?

Who cops out? The one who despairs of American totalitarianism and imperialism and heists the banner of Hanoi, Moscow, Peking, or Havana? Or the one who sees that the same technique of principalities and powers is at work in all governments and that it is God who sits above the circle of the earth, God who brings the princes of the earth to nothing and judges our governments as he judges us, by what we do to the children, the prisoners, the whores, the addicts, the scared, the bewildered, the poor, the hungry—to "the least of them" who is the one we call Lord! Lord!?

Who cops out? The Institute of the Prophets of the King of Israel? Or Micaiah son of Imlah?

* * *

But why do we address ourselves to you, Dr. Graham? Maybe it is because you are our Baptist brother, and we love you. Or maybe because, as students of liberal and Ivy League divinity and graduate schools a decade or so ago, we opposed and scorned those who, early in your career, haughtily and with snickers barred you from their Common Rooms and Chapels. We opposed them at the time because we thought, despite your lack of the Ivy League specialties we were then seeking (erudition and academic degrees), that you were a man preaching more Jesus than culture, more gospel than law. We were finding that quality sadly lacking in our own theological preparation, as was more than evident when you were banned from speaking to us as our guest and brother in Christ.

And so maybe we are now just a little hurt and peeved to see a man we once tried to stand up for become more and more a man of tremendous power and influence. Maybe we cannot accept your use of that power and influence, in Christ's name, to become a court prophet in the tradition of Zedekiah son of Kenaanah, adding your blessing (and power) to the current kings of Israel and Judah—whether in the semi-secrecy of a political convention corridor in California, the pages of *Life* magazine, the records of your innermost prayers about political maneuvering on the national level, or on the golf course, in Neyland Stadium at the University of Tennessee, at the East Room of the White House. And whether it is Lyndon Johnson, Richard Nixon, George Wallace, or George McGovern you press to your bosom. Whether it is "busing" in North Carolina or "winning" in Vietnam you speak about in your interviews and sermons.

Maybe it's because we can no longer accept in your ministry the very thing we rejected in the ministry of our liberal and Ivy League brothers: the worship of politics; the whoring-up to political gods, leaders, powers, and principalities; the service to the Baals in the chicanery, flimflam, deceit, and murder that defines the present political process; the confession Christian leaders make that "God is dead" when we are enjoined to obey "the

law" whether we like it or not, even though we render to
Caesar what is God's and to God what is Caesar's, and do
so as an act of faith.

Maybe it is all or any of these things.

But we believe it is something else. We believe that the
connection between your power and influence and what
you say to and about the kings of Israel and Judah must
be broken. For the best example of what we mean, we
believe that the only way you, or any of us, can *minister*
to the troops and inhabitants of Vietnam is *to prophesy*
to the Pentagon and White House—in the tradition of
Micaiah son of Imlah.

And you, our brother, have been and will be the
prophet summoned to those halls. We shall not. So, in
love, we remind you, our brother, of what you have so
often proclaimed:

"The Bible says that. . . ."

> 1 For three years there was no war between the Ara-
> maeans and the Israelites.
>
> 2 But in the third year Jehoshaphat king of Judah went
> down to visit the king of Israel.
>
> 3 The latter said to his courtiers, "You know that Ra-
> moth-gilead belongs to us, and yet we do nothing to recover
> it from the king of Aram."
>
> 4 He said to Jehoshaphat, "Will you join me in attacking
> Ramoth-gilead?" Jehoshaphat said to the king of Israel,
> "What is mine is yours; myself, my people, and my horses."
>
> 5 Then Jehoshaphat said to the king of Israel, "First let us
> seek counsel from the Lord."
>
> 6 The king of Israel assembled the prophets, some four
> hundred of them, and asked them, "Shall I attack Ramoth-
> gilead or shall I refrain?" "Attack," they answered; "the
> Lord will deliver it into your hands."
>
> 7 Jehoshaphat asked, "Is there no other prophet of the
> Lord here through whom we may seek guidance?"
>
> 8 "There is one more," the king of Israel answered,
> "through whom we may seek guidance of the Lord, but I
> hate the man, because he prophesies no good for me; never

anything but evil. His name is Micaiah son of Imlah." Jehoshaphat exclaimed, "My lord king, let no such word pass your lips!"

9 So the king of Israel called one of his eunuchs and told him to fetch Micaiah son of Imlah with all speed.

10 The king of Israel and Jehoshaphat king of Judah were seated on their thrones, in shining armor, at the entrance of the gate of Samaria, and all the prophets were prophesying before them.

11 One of them, Zedekiah son of Kenaanah, made himself horns of iron and said, "This is the word of the Lord: 'With horns like these you shall gore the Aramaeans and make an end of them.' "

12 In the same vein all the prophets prophesied, "Attack Ramoth-gilead and win the day; the Lord will deliver it into your hands."

13 The messenger sent to fetch Micaiah told him that the prophets had with one voice given the king a favorable answer. "And mind you agree with them," he added.

14 "As the Lord lives," said Micaiah, "I will say only what the Lord tells me to say."

15 When Micaiah came into the king's presence, the king said to him, "Micaiah, shall we attack Ramoth-gilead or shall we refrain?" "Attack and win the day," he said; "the Lord will deliver it into your hands."

16 "How often must I adjure you," said the king, "to tell me nothing but the truth in the name of the Lord."

17 Then Micaiah said, "I saw all Israel scattered on the mountains, like sheep without a shepherd; and I heard the Lord say, 'They have no master, let them go home in peace.' "

18 The king of Israel said to Jehoshaphat, "Did I not tell you that he never prophesies good for me, nothing but evil?"

19 Micaiah went on, "Listen now to the word of the Lord. I saw the Lord seated on his throne, with all the host of heaven in attendance on his right and on his left.

20 The Lord said, 'Who will entice Ahab to attack and fall at Ramoth-gilead?' One said one thing and one said another;

21 Then a spirit came forward and stood before the Lord and said, 'I will entice him.'

22 'How?' said the Lord. 'I will go out and be a lying spirit in the mouth of all his prophets.' 'You shall entice him,' said the Lord, 'and you shall succeed; go and do it.'

23 You see, then, how the Lord has put a lying spirit in the mouth of all these prophets of yours, because he has decreed disaster for you."

24 Then Zedekiah son of Kenaanah came up to Micaiah and struck him in the face: "And how did the spirit of the Lord pass from me to speak to you?" he said.

25 Micaiah answered, "That you will find out on the day when you run into an inner room and hide yourself."

26 Then the king of Israel ordered Micaiah to be arrested and committed to the custody of Amon the governor of the city and Joash the king's son.

27 "Lock this fellow up," he said, "and give him prison diet of bread and water until I come home in safety."

28 Micaiah retorted, "If you do return in safety, the Lord has not spoken by me."

29 So the king of Israel and Jehoshaphat king of Judah marched on Ramoth-gilead, and the King of Israel said to Jehoshaphat,

30 "I will disguise myself to go into battle, but you shall wear your royal robes." So he went into battle in disguise.

31 Now the king of Aram had commanded the thirty-two captains of his chariots not to engage all the sundry but the king of Israel alone.

32 When the captains saw Jehoshaphat, they thought he was the king of Israel and turned to attack him.

33 But Jehoshaphat cried out and, when the captains saw that he was not the king of Israel, they broke off the attack on him.

34 But one man drew his bow at random and hit the king of Israel where the breastplate joins the plates of the armor. So he said to his driver, "Wheel round and take me out of the line; I am wounded."

35 When the day's fighting reached its height, the king

was facing the Aramaeans propped up in his chariot, and the blood from his wound flowed down upon the floor of the chariot; and in the evening he died.

36 At sunset the herald went through the ranks, crying, "Every man to his city, every man to his country." Thus died the king.

37 He was brought to Samaria and they buried him there.

38 The chariot was swilled out at the pool of Samaria, and the dogs licked up the blood, and the prostitutes washed themselves in it, in fulfilment of the word the Lord had spoken.

I Kings 22:1-38

Yes, Brother! The Bible says. . . !

Sincerely, your brothers,

Will D. Campbell
James Y. Holloway

9

Annihilating the Hillbilly:
The Appalachians' Struggle
with America's Institutions
JAMES G. BRANSCOME

Not too long ago, CBS television featured, back-to-back, on Tuesday nights, three of America's most popular TV programs: "The Beverly Hillbillies," "Green Acres," and "Hee-Haw." This combination has to be the most intensive effort ever exerted by a nation to belittle, demean, and otherwise destroy a minority people within its boundaries. Within the three shows on one night, hillbillies were shown being conned into buying the White House, coddling a talking pig, and rising from a cornpatch to crack the sickest jokes on TV—all on the same channel, all only a short while after Eric Sevareid completed his nightly lecture to the American public on decency, integrity, dignity, and the other great American virtues to which he and his network supposedly adhere.

JAMES G. BRANSCOME is Director of Save Our Kentucky (SOK), an organization seeking to abolish strip-mining. For several years he was Director, Youth Opportunities Project, Appalachian Regional Commission. He is a member of the Editorial Board of *Katallagete.*

If similar programs even approaching the maliciousness of these were broadcast on Blacks, Indians, or Chicanos, there would be an immediate public outcry from every liberal organization and politician in the country and a scathing editorial in the *New York Times* about the programs' "lack of taste." The new culture people would organize marches and prime-time boycotts and perhaps, even, throw dog dung at Eva Gabor as she emerged from her studio. They might even go a step further and deal with that hillybilly-maligning patriot, Al Capp. But, with this, as all things Appalachian, *silence.* America is allowed to continue laughing at this minority group because on this, America agrees: hillbilly ain't beautiful.

The treatment given by the media to Appalachia is only one example of the massive failure of America's institutions for over a century to meet the needs of the people of the region. From government at all levels, to churches, private welfare agencies, schools, colleges, labor unions, foundations, newspapers, corporations, *ad infinitum*, the region has received an unequal share of exploitation, neglect, unfulfilled promises and misguided assistance. This is not to deny that America is interested in Appalachia. It has been for some time, in the peculiar American way—in Appalachia's worth to industry, of course; only erratically in the plight of the people. General Howard of the Freedman's Bureau is said to have convinced Lincoln that he ought to try to do something for the poor mountaineers after the Civil War. The New Deal brought the then rather progressive Tennessee Valley Authority to one part of the region, but TVA's recently developed capacity to burn lower-grade strip-mine coal brought the hellish human and material waste of that process to Central Appalachia. John Kennedy and his brother Robert both professed an interest in the hillbilly and his vote, and eventually, under Lyndon Johnson, their interest was translated into the Appalachian Regional Commission, a unique political and economic development agency. But, as Harry Caudill remarked, its assignment was "one of the most awesome tasks since Hercules cleaned the Augean stables."

It is especially Herculean when one applies some good American economic analysis: the agency was given about *one-twentieth* of the amount of money it takes to fight the Vietnam war *for one year* and told to use that amount over a *six-year period* to correct almost two hundred years of abuse to areas of a thirteen-state region! Now, for the riddle: if eighty percent of that money was spent on highway construction, how interested is America in the nineteen million people who occupy the territory the Commission described in 1964 "as an island of poverty in a sea of affluence"? This is not to deny that the Commission has not had a positive influence on the region. Given the parameters in which it had to work, it has made many needed investments in public facilities and increased the accountability of state governments to their Appalachian sections. If Congress extends the program and significantly increases its funding for human resource programs, the Commission may be able to bring to the Appalachian poor some of the services even ghetto residents have come to accept as normal. There are some big *ifs* in this, not the least of which is the critical question today about the relationship between institutions and people: *if* an institution today had unlimited funding and unlimited maneuverability, could it bring to people the services they need without destroying the kind of life they want to live?

If the ability of institutions to respond to people's needs is judged on the basis of the Federal Government's enforcement of the Mine Health and Safety Act of 1969, then the answer to this question is *No!* Loud and Clear. The death of the 78 coal miners in Farmington, West Virginia, in November 1968 led to the passage of that act, which is the strictest mine safety legislation ever to get through Congress and be signed by a President. The public outrage over Farmington gave government one of its few opportunities to wrestle successfully with the powerful American coal-oil conglomerates. But, something did not work: either there is no will, or desire, by the bureaucracies (*the* institutions) of the Federal Government to go to the mat with the conglomerates. Perhaps their interests are so inseparable that no contest is ever possible. In any case: since the disaster, more than 700 miners have been killed *in the mines* and more than 10,000 have been crippled or injured. There has been no public outcry to avenge the death of these men.

Moreover, the Social Security Administration's own Bureau of Disability Insurance provides some statistics to indicate how the bureaucracy of one fundamental institution—government—deals with one crisis that the 1969 Act sought to meet: compensation for miners disabled by "black lung" contracted after long years and long hours inside the mines. The national average of claims under the black lung provisions of the Act processed by the Bureau of Disability Insurance is 43%. However, only 22% of the claims from eastern Kentucky and 24% of those from West Virginia had been processed by early November 1970. And 52% of the processed claims of West Virginia miners have been denied; 71% of Kentucky miners have been denied. The figure for claims denied for the rest of the nation is only 20%.

If one reflects on the fact that in the past seventy years there have been 101,000 mine deaths, a number larger than the total of miners now working in Appalachia, and double the number of Vietnam deaths, then the inability of the government to enforce regulations, which are mild by international comparison, strikes one as not speaking well for the capacity of political institutions to use the very arena of action which is theirs, by democracy's mandate, or for the American public's capacity to care for anything more than the dramatic, never the substantial.

And with the death of thirty-eight men in the Finley mines near Hyden, Kentucky, on December 30, 1970, the nation was once again reminded about the plight of miners in Appalachian coal pits. The President of the United States himself announced that he would have visited the scene of the disaster . . . if it had not been for "the bad weather." (Yet no airports in the region were closed.) The more important visits, however—those of inspectors from the Bureau of Mines—had not been made on schedule some few days before the disaster in order to check correction of violations of the 1969 act cited on earlier visits. It was the same old refrain: new priority guidelines for violations under the new act had just come down from Washington to the Bureau's regional office in eastern Kentucky, necessitating a new schedule of visits; the office itself was short-handed because some of the inspectors had taken "Christmas leave"; the mine operators complained that some provisions of the act were a peril to the safety of miners and mines; no one, not even the inspectors, understood all of the provisions of the act. Etc. Etc. In any event, the Finley mines were permitted to operate up to the disaster on December 30. They did so in large part because an inspection required under the 1969 act was subjected to the administration of a bureaucracy which, perhaps unwittingly but in fact, vetoed the will and intention of the Congress and the President and—if representative government is still taken seriously—the will of the people. Thirty-eight men dead. And the litany of charges: families of the dead miners exploited by funeral operators, insurance claim men, and government officials; cover-ups and double-dealings and politics involved in the "hearings" to inquire into the disaster; illegal "prime-cord" and "dynamite" had (and had not) been used in the mines; an inspector "who didn't want his name used" said a simultaneous explosion ten times the legal limit was set off when the men were killed. . . .

The complete failure of the American corporate structure to accept even a charitable responsibility for the region that it has raped so successfully is hardly arguable. Since men like General Imboden in the late nineteenth century went before the state legislatures to argue that ". . . within the imperial domain of Virginia, lie, almost unknown to the outside world and not fully appreciated by their owners, vaster fields of coal and iron than in all England, maybe, than all Europe," the American corporate community has wrenched resources estimated at a worth of nearly one trillion dollars from the mountains. While these companies pay some of the highest dividends of any company in the world to their already wealthy shareholders, the *communities* in Appalachia where those resources originated survive on a subsistence economy—if "survive" is the proper verb here. Often more than half of the money in circulation comes from state and federal welfare coffers. This fact alone tells us something about the American Way, if not the American Dream. Three months after the June 30, 1970, deadline for reducing the amount of hazardous dust in the mines as required by the 1969 legislation, 2800 of the 3000 underground mine operators had not complied. These same companies have continually opposed severance taxes on coal and medical benefits for the more than 100,000 disabled miners who suffer permanent lung damage from poorly maintained mines. Apparently when these corporate institutions of American free enterprise become incredibly wealthy, they cannot be expected to have conscience even to allow *government* to pay the tab for the damage they have caused. Somewhere that "pursuit of selfish interest accruing benefits to all" went astray in Appalachia.

* * *

It has always been asserted with pride that America takes great interest in its children. "Dr. Spock" has been a best-seller for over a decade. But this "child-dominated" society has interest only in certain children. Of the more than 925,000 poor children under six in Appalachia, as estimated by the Office of Economic Opportunity, only about 100,000 receive cash benefits in their home from Aid to Dependent Children or other similar welfare programs. The national participation rate of children in Head Start programs decreased three percent between 1967 and 1969; the Appalachian participation decreased fifteen percent. The greatest decrease in Appalachia, significantly, was in full-year programs, those regarded as most beneficial to poor children. What other group in the country received the benefits from the cutbacks in Appalachia is unimportant here; that "hillbillies" were not on the priority list is obvious.

In the area of prenatal and infant care, the situation in Appalachia is even more alarming. Examinations of children in several areas of the region have shown that as many as seventy percent have "parasitic infestation" (the euphemism for "worms"), one of the causes contributing to Appalachia's unusually large number of retarded and "slow" children—"worms" abounding in the miserable shacks and grassless yards American free enterprise has put aside for the hillbillies. If the Appalachian infant mortality rate were reduced at the same rate as East Germany's in a five-year period (as reported by the World Health Organization), the lives of more than 1,000 children a year could be preserved. In certain areas of the region, as a matter of fact, the situation worsened over a decade. In Lamar County, Alabama, for example, the infant mortality rate rose from 32.5 percent to 40.9 percent in ten years. The rate in Hancock County, Tennessee, rose from 21.4 percent to 42.2 percent in the same time period. While increased attention to child development at the national and regional level promises to better the situation, for many lives and for many minds the help comes too late. Perhaps if it were possible to estimate the number of mountain children who would be alive and healthy if Appalachia had received and retained a more equitable share of the nation's wealth, certain institutions could be persuaded more easily to invest in saving children. Until the case is made, however, we all labor under the curse of the prophets and the admonitions of the poets (increasingly, it seems, the only sane people), that the final judgment on civilizations and their institutions rests on how well they treat their children, who are—in appeal at least—the "least of these."

The Appalachian child who makes it to school does not find the institution America has charged with equipping youth with basic "survival" skills any better prepared to serve his needs. The inability and unwillingness of local governments to tax the property and extractive resources of large corporations have resulted in an educational system in Appalachia that can only be compared with that in the so-called "underdeveloped" nations. Add to this the fundamental resistance of middle-class teachers to acknowledge the unique cultural heritage of the Appalachian youth, and you have a laboratory for studying one of the classic historical struggles between a nation intent on erasing a minority from its midst and a people intent on preserving their identity and life-style at any cost to themselves. In an Appalachian school, the middle-class, aspiring teacher is just as insistent that the student be aggressive, obedient, joyless—in short, everything that his culture tells him he is not—as is the teacher in the Bureau of Indian Affairs school on a reservation. No wonder, then, that as many as 65 percent of the students drop out of school before graduation—a figure 25 percent higher than the national average.

Responding to the fiscal needs of the Appalachian educational system alone is overwhelmingly beyond the capacity of government agencies as they are presently funded. In 1967, for example, the Office of Education estimated that the construction needs of the thirteen

Appalachian states represented over 42 percent of the total school construction needs of the entire country. It would require the additional expenditure of $363 million annually just to raise the per pupil expenditures of Appalachian schools to the national average. Title I of the Elementary and Secondary Education Act, designed to increase the amount of funds available for the teaching of disadvantaged students, will spend more money on an equal number of students in the schools of Westchester, New York, where the number of poor students is about three percent of the student body, than it will in a county in Appalachia where more than half of the student body is poor. Talent Search, a special college recruitment and placement program funded by Congress for high-risk students, spends only 3.8 percent of its money in Appalachia, compared to the 10 percent the region deserves. Simply to make the Appalachian educational system equal in educational resources to the nation will require a political miracle at a time when no miracle workers are to be found.

While Appalachia is heavily populated with institutions of higher learning supported by various religious denominations and state governments, the region's students are no better served here than in the secondary institutions. Neither is the region's needs for professional and paraprofessional manpower. No institution of American society, in fact, is more divorced from Appalachia than the higher educational system residing within it.

Forced by accrediting agencies, visiting boards, and hundreds of other pressures to maintain a facade of "academic excellence" and "a sound liberal arts education," usually with Christ thrown in somewhere, the church-supported schools spend little time thinking about the community below their own mountainside. Their emphasis on admitting Appalachian students is so small, their tuition so high, and pressure so intense from church supporters outside the region to admit their sons and daughters, that most of these colleges have an inordinately high percentage of students from states like New Jersey. Certainly to these colleges, "Christian" education has nothing to do with serving the victims of Caesar's educational system.

The "open door" policies of state universities are often, in actuality, "revolving doors" for the Appalachian student. Once the student is admitted and the fees collected (either from him or the state), the more aggressive and well-trained student from another section of the state or nation, and the freshman composition teacher, can be expected to send the Appalachian student scurrying home. In January 1968 the National Association of State Universities and Land Grant Colleges summed up the record of their members in the region with: "To maintain quality they raised student charges substantially, turned away qualified students, limited enrollments, and refused urgently needed public services."

The regional universities and colleges place little emphasis on promoting a regional consciousness on the part of their students. In fact, there is not at present a single Appalachian studies program in the region which could begin to rival the offerings in Far Eastern studies or astronomy. One, Eastern Kentucky University in Richmond (which in reality is in "Blue Grass," not "eastern," Kentucky) prides itself on its training and research in law enforcement and police work. All this continues and intensifies a channeling process begun by the elementary teacher to send the Appalachian student—ashamed of his background and ill-equipped to meet the needs of his region—into middle-class society outside the region. The sixteen-year process of credentializing to which the student has been subjected finally becomes a ticket to the world of Dick and Jane, Support-Your-Local-Police, and the affluence of America built at Appalachia's expense. So a region that needs more than 200,000 college graduates—a minimum of 5,000 physicians, many more thousands of nurses, teachers, businessmen, government leaders, *ad infinitum*—finds no help in another of America's institutions.

The young Appalachian left behind by the higher educational system is destined to be the object of a number of complicated channeling devices. The male youth, if he can pass the examinations, is eligible for one of the more obvious youth channeling programs in the country, the Army. Selective Service does not maintain records on Appalachians as a group, but the number in the service is estimated to be higher than their percentage in the population because the armed forces represent the only opportunity available to many young mountain men to be assimilated into mainline America. Recent Department of Defense figures report that West Virginia led the nation in per capita Vietnam deaths. *Twenty-five* West Virginians per 100,000 population had been killed, compared to *seventeen* per 100,000 nationally.

For the youth who seeks opportunity and training in some special opportunity program, such as the Job Corps, the fate may not be a great deal more encouraging. Because of the Job Corps' resistance to establishing a center especially for Appalachian youth, they are sent to camps, both within and outside the region, where the population may be largely urban and black. Combine his unfamiliarity with urban life and blacks with his affinity for home and family, and one can easily understand why the Appalachian youth drops out of the program in equal frequency with his Indian counterpart. Even if he lasts the program out, according to Joint Action in Community Service, the agency that contracts with the Job Corps to place and counsel graduates, it is very difficult to find him a job or to locate a person or agency willing to assist him in the mountains.

For the youth who has not dropped out of school by the ninth grade and who has no prospect of attending college, vocational training represents the only channel open to him. Many find it a wicked channel indeed. Three years ago the Education Advisory Committee of the Appalachian Regional Commission reported that half of all vocational training programs in the region consisted of agriculture and home economics—areas in which there were almost no job openings. Since that report the Commission and the states have required all 235 vocational programs which they have funded to teach job-relevant skills. While only half of the schools are now open and no thorough evaluation has been reported, it is expected that the schools will be significantly better than their predecessors.

As late as 1968, however, the West Virginia Commission on Higher Education reported that only about 18 percent of the students in that state had access to vocational training. Given the fact that post-high school vocational training is still not available to the majority of Appalachian youth, this major channel of supposed opportunity still has a long way to go to overcome the serious handicaps it has represented in the past. And with improvement, vocational education's role may be to channel all the so-called disadvantaged students into neat slots, thereby diminishing not only the student, but vocational education as well. Additionally, so long as vocational school graduates must leave the mountains to find jobs, the region will remain a loser. It is already estimated that 900,000 high school graduates will have to leave the region to find jobs in the 1970s. They will thus become the people the cities do not want and the people the region cannot afford to lose.

The fact that a mountain youth takes advantage of the opportunity to finish high school and apply to college does not guarantee that the tentacles of the system will let him go. For instance, one of the high-risk students I taught in the Upward Bound program at Berea College applied and was accepted in the fall at that college. During the preceding spring he was approached by a recruiter for the FBI who gave him a hard sell on the benefits of working for the Bureau in Washington. He dropped the idea of college and is now a low-paid clerk at FBI head-quarters. Since this incident I have checked with school personnel in other areas of the region and found that intensive recruitment of high school graduates in rural areas is now carried out by the FBI and other government agencies who are not finding recruits for their clerk and typist posts in urban high schools. The law, it seems, has a long arm and no qualms about modern forms of im-pressment.

Most high school dropouts—except those who marry and somehow find work or welfare payments—and unem-ployed high school graduates eventually end up being forced to migrate to find work. In West Virginia, for instance, 70 percent of the young people leave before they reach the age of 24. Usually referred to as "mi-grants" instead of more accurately as economic refugees, these youth join the more than 3,000,000 other moun-taineers who have preceded them to northern cities such as Cincinnati, Chicago, Indianapolis, and Detroit since World War II. If they have a skill and happen to move during a period of relative economic prosperity, or are willing to accept a job run by the stopwatch and a minimum-wage employer, as many do, their chances for survival are good. If, on the other hand, they have to move in with kin in the "back home" ghetto, the situa-tion is different.

The unemployed and unassimilated mountain youth finds himself in a bewildering ghetto that defies descrip-tion, and usually comparison, with the ghetto life of other minorities. He also finds that in the city there is one thing more unacceptable than a black man—a hill-billy, a ridgerunner, a briarhopper. For the first time in its history America has recognized him as a cultural minority. If he ends up in juvenile court for stealing hubcaps, he is offered leniency with his promise to go "back home." Judges make this offer to youth whose families may have been in the city for three generations and can only consider themselves Cincinnatians or Chicagoans. If he enters school, studies show that its foreign nature drives him out faster both psychologically and physically than it does his black migrant counterpart. For the mountain youth who is unable or unwilling to assimilate into the life of the city, there is little help from the social service agencies who understand much more about blacks than they do about him. He is thus not only without help, but—perhaps more appallingly—without an advocate in a city that he does not understand and that does not understand him.

One group of Appalachians who are consistently over-looked and underserved by the institutions of the region are the blacks. As a matter of fact, both government and the so-called "private" welfare agencies refuse to acknowl-edge the existence of blacks in Appalachia. While the percentage of blacks in the region as a whole is low—about eight percent—they make up the entire population of many small, isolated hollows and ghost coal towns abandoned by the corporations and welfare and poverty agencies. Because the backbreaking jobs that brought black imports into the region are gone and because of the discrimination and competition with the majority of poor white people for jobs and welfare funds, their existence is a poor one, indeed. As yet no agency report or journalist has documented the presence and needs of these people, let alone described the culture of a minority group in the midst of another cultural minority.

* * *

America's unwillingness to deal with the Appalachian as he asks to be dealt with is probably no more baffling than America's seeming obsession to study and under-

stand his unusual life-style and values. Even before the
Russell Sage Foundation published John Campbell's *The
Southern Highlander and His Homeland* in 1921, writers
and sociologists were making forays into the mountains
alternately to praise, condemn, and collect the mountain
culture. The studies are still being made today in the
midst of the technological revolution that is, for all
practical purposes, making "Middle Americans" all alike.
The conclusions of modern studies do not differ from
those made in the last century. The Appalachian is different: he is existence-oriented, independent, has close
family ties, is fatalistic, cares for his elderly, *ad nauseam.*
If, as Robert Coles and others have written of late, the
Appalachian has a life-style, a culture, that America
would do well to listen to, if not opt for, why has
America failed so miserably at times to meet his needs?

Part of the answer is obviously that Appalachia has
been in the main a colonial territory for America within
her own boundaries. The life-style of the region served
well the need of the mining and lumbering corporations
for a subjugated people willing to be peasants in their
own land. Even after the bloody struggles to unionize the
mines, the capacity of America's institutions (including
its labor unions) to contain the people's struggle remained intact. So what on the surface appear to be
quaint people, to be explained away by their isolation
and independence, may, in fact, be more accurately described as the historical reaction of the people to colonialism.

What on the surface may strike Jack Weller, author of
Yesterday's People (published jointly by the University
of Kentucky and the Council of the Southern Mountains), as ignorance that keeps people from taking polio
shots even when they are offered free transportation,
may, in fact, be better explained by Frantz Fanon, a
physician himself, who argued (in *The Wretched of the
Earth*) that the Algerians resisted "modern medical tech-

niques" so long as the French were in control of them, but adopted the new practices immediately when they felt themselves to be in control. I have seen parents who refused to have their children vaccinated at the public health clinic, willingly have them vaccinated when it was "our" medical students who were giving the shots.

One has to understand how the medical profession in Appalachia operates to appreciate fully this phenomenon. He has to sit with a young father in the mountains and hear the story of how his pregnant, now deceased, wife was turned away from the hospital because he did not have the hundred dollars that the doctors demand as a down payment for those who do not have medical insurance. It is these same compassionate physicians who have, rather than reform their own practices to meet the needs of people, turned the Medicaid program into a thriving business. The potential earning from the health support programs is so great that a recent government report on physician manpower in Appalachia suggested that it was one of the most lucrative enticements to get doctors into the region—another colonial characteristic. A largely overlooked article in the Louisville *Courier-Journal* in the spring of 1970 described how doctors and pharmacists have turned Medicaid recipients in eastern Kentucky into addicts and junkies. It repeated reports from law officers and nurses who had seen "whole families lying around in a stupor" and "glassy-eyed teenagers and small children wobbling or passed out along the roadside" because they took narcotics prescribed by their physicians. One eastern Kentucky pharmacist admitted that 65 percent of his business came from Medicaid dues. "The poor people are substituting pills for faith," he explained. He went on to describe why the abuses are allowed to continue: "It would cost the pharmacist a great deal in time away from work to keep a check on abuses. They are just too busy."

By and large American institutions can be said, then,

to have held no respect for the mountaineer other than for his use as an object. Richard Davis notes in his recent *The Man Who Moved a Mountain* (Fortress Press), large metropolitan newspapers used the notorious Allen feud of the second decade of this century in Hillsville, Virginia, to interpret the Appalachian to their urban readers. Said one:

> The majority of mountain people are unprincipled ruffians. They make moonshine, 500 horsepower, and swill it down; they carry on generous and gentle feuds in which little children are not spared, and deliberately plan a wholesale assassination, and when captured either assert they shot in self-defense, or with true coward streak deny the crime. There are two remedies only—education or extermination. Mountaineers, like the red Indian, must learn this lesson.

Another editorial in a northern newspaper on the same event went on to conclude:

> The Scotch-Irish mountaineers are more ignorant than vicious, victims of heredity and alcohol, and now that their isolated region has been invaded, must change or perish.

One of the often overlooked aspects of the outsiders' fetish for Appalachia has been the premises that underlie their own prescriptions for the people's future. One finds in Jack Weller's influential writings, for instance, comments such as these:

> There is little in the mountain child's training that would help him develop self-control, discipline, resolution, or steadfastness. Thus the way is prepared for future difficulties in the army or at work.

> Since the culture inadequately prepares its members to relate to "outsiders," there is a great need for "bridge" persons, who can help the suspicious and fearful to respond more positively to persons and institutions which will increasingly be of help and resource—doctors, psychiatrists, clinics, hospitals, government in the form of agency officials,

policemen, public health nurses, welfare workers, and recreation leaders. The mountaineer's suspicion of these persons limits his use of them to crisis occasions, when, in fact, their purpose is to be of assistance in many ways at other times. He needs help in understanding that government and other institutions cannot be run in person-oriented ways but must be conducted in great measure on an impersonal objective basis. He needs help in seeing that a certain amount of bureaucratic organization is a necessary thing, and that a government does not exist for an individual person's benefit (*Yesterday's People*, pp. 157-158).

Responding to the Appalachian culture, outsiders are sometimes incapable of interpreting the evidence because of their own training in research procedures. One, for example (while, of course, repeatedly enjoining his readers that he is passing no judgment on the culture), describes mountain music and literature as "regressive looking," "nostalgic and melancholy," over all, "repressive." Thomas Merton, on the other hand, after hearing some mountain music for the first time at the Abbey of Gethsemani, gave the correct interpretation and exclaimed, "It's apocalyptic!" Perhaps the only fair hearing the culture of the people of Appalachia will receive is from persons like mystics and contemplatives who do not assign ultimate importance to the things that the modern state and today's seminarians have blessed as divine.

The churchmen, educators, welfare agents, independent do-gooders, journalists, and novelists, and the institutions which pay their salaries—that is, those who have made an extraordinarily good living trying to "understand" the mountain man—have studied the Appalachian not to learn from him, but rather to "teach" him, to "school" him, to "doctor" and "save" him by making him into what they already are: Middle America, assimilated into the America of the television and Holiday Inn—the America which Tocqueville and Faulkner warned was founded by those who sought not to escape from tyranny, but to establish one, in their own image and likeness.

Only in Appalachia, for example, have the mainline churches come upon a "Christian" religious expression which stands four-square against what they expect religion in America to "do." The rejection of the "Christian century" by Appalachia has baffled and annoyed the mainline churches, their agencies, theologians, and sociologists. And because the church in mainline America is unable to understand the church in Appalachia, it has so far been unable to assimilate it. It has failed, in other words, to make it over into another of the agencies of social welfare alongside HEW, Social Security, the Council of the Southern Mountains, the Commission on Religion in Appalachia, the Home Mission Board(s), etc. The mainline churches have tried to obliterate the Appalachian churches with demands for expressions which are "progressive," "rational," "contemporary" and "relevant." What more haunting, and in many instances disgusting, examples of the philosopher's "ambiguity of reason" or the theologian's "original sin" could be asked for? The liberal churchmen—Catholic and Protestant—insist that the snake handling of the mountain man must come to an end (as must the "emotionalism" and "irrelevance" of the black church). And all the while the mainline, liberal church ignores the more dangerous "snake handling" which defines their very efforts to "save" "yesterday's people"—a phenomenon described precisely by Thomas Merton in "Events and Pseudo-Events: Letter to a Southern Churchman" (see above, pp. 78-94).

* * *

The answer to the question why mountain culture must be destroyed is to be found in the fundamental truth about the technological society: the techniques which undergird all our institutions are assimilating all of us into, as Jacques Ellul puts it, "a society of objects, run by objects." Institutions in the technological society—and this means not only those of the state and its welfare bureaus, but the do-good agencies which include churches, schools, and colleges—can respond only by and with the techniques of the impersonalized, bureaucratic means, procedures, formulas. Technique cannot discriminate between right and wrong, justice and injustice. That is why the same technique that gives (and takes away) the health card from an ailing miner, assimilates the pious mountaineer into the five-point grading system and the Uniform Sunday School Lesson.

The meaning is clear: institutions working in Appalachia today can work for only *one* end: the extinction of the Appalachian people. The extent to which these institutions have so far failed in the venture is the extent to which this people and culture have successfully resisted the formidable pressures of the institutions of contemporary technological society. Why institutions—political and private, church and business, industrial and charitable—have responded and can respond to the Appalachian the way they have tells us something very important about power—and powerlessness—in the technological society.

For those of us who believe that the struggle is for the soul of man in the technological society, the resistance of Appalachian culture against assimilation into middle America demands earnest, indeed prayerful, attention. The struggle of the mountain man against the institutions of the technological society is the struggle to deny their right to define any man by his relationship to Middle America. The struggle—whether one believes that it comes out of resistance informed by left-wing Protestantism or opposition to colonialism and genocide—has implications for all who question not only the possibility, but the quality and character of any resistance to the totalitarianism of the technological society.

10

In Defense of the Steeple

DUNCAN GRAY, JR.

The parish church has taken lots of abuse in recent years and is, in large measure, an object of contempt for many within the church as well as outside it. It is considered obsolete and outmoded; indeed, *dead*, in a sociological sense, as well as in a spiritual sense. Many clergy, frustrated by the forces of conservatism, tradition, and "respectability," are leaving the parish ministry; and many seminarians hope for some other channel through which to give themselves to their Lord and their church. (A recent survey in my own communion indicated that only 45% of the men in seminary today want to exercise their ministry in a parish situation!)

In no area of concern is the criticism more pointed—or more justified—than in the area of race relations. Here the failure of the parish church in the white community is most evident, and to try to document this failure would simply be a matter of proclaiming the obvious. The

DUNCAN GRAY, JR., is rector of St. Paul's Episcopal Church in Meridian, Mississippi. He is past president of the Mississippi Council of human relations and a member of the Editorial Board of *Katallagete*.

average parish church remains one of the last strongholds of segregation, and significant leadership in this area has been sadly lacking.

While not unmindful of the weaknesses and failures of the parish, and sensitive, I trust, to the validity of so much of the criticism leveled against it, I am not yet ready to throw up my hands in despair over the local church. To be sure, other vehicles of ministry and mission are needed badly; but I see these growing up and bearing fruit alongside of and in addition to the parish church, rather than replacing it. Indeed, this is already happening on a significant scale, for which we can give thanks to God. But in our passion for new and more effective forms of ministry, let us not relegate every St. John's-By-the-Fire-Station to the junk heap. There are yet many resources to be tapped in the parish church for witnessing to and making effective the reconciliation of men to God and men to men. More to the point, the parish church may be the one place where this can be done in any final or meaningful way.

Let us confess, first of all, that the parish church as an institution is not a very effective instrument of social change, much less of social revolution. Being a family-oriented institution, it is inevitably conservative in nature and make-up. We won't find many local congregations, *as congregations,* "manning the barricades," marching in the streets, or sitting in at the Congress, either now or in the future. The involvement of Christians in this kind of activity will be as individuals or as part of some specialized vehicle of ministry and mission. All of which may be quite proper and necessary.

But two things must be remembered about this form of witness. First, under even the best of circumstances, it will involve relatively few people; and, secondly, as essential as it may be, this in itself is not going to bring in the millennium or anything approximating the Kingdom of

God. We have enough laws, court decisions, and executive orders in effect already to bring about reconciliation between white and black, *if* such could be accomplished by these alone. And yet the degree of separation and alienation seems to be greater than ever before. As important as legal action may be, it still does not get to the heart of the matter: the matter of the human heart.

I am well aware that changing institutions can change people—to a degree. We see many a white Mississippian who only a few short years ago was vowing that "blood would run in the streets" before one Negro child would enter one white school in his community, now taking in stride the black classmates with whom his sons and daughters associate every day and even cheering lustily for them on the football field and elsewhere. But the man himself has changed little. Psychologically, he is as estranged as ever from his black brethren. He has gained a measure of tolerance in certain areas—which is all to the good—but he is still not ready to accept the Negro as his equal and as his brother. Things keep on changing, but somehow they still remain the same.

The Kerner Report says that after all our legislating, politicking, and moralizing of recent years, we still find in America the evil of "white racism" at the heart of our disorder, violence, and alienation. (And this, of course, has produced a "black racism" which only intensifies the problem.) And we know that this is the racism, not just of the Ku Kluxer, but of nearly all of us, even including many who have worked for and voted for the laws that were supposed to deliver us. Where do we go to solve *this* problem? What resources do we have to deal with it, when the resources of law and politics are being exhausted so rapidly?

First of all, we go *where the people are*. And in Bible-Belt Mississippi, at least, this means we go to the parish church. The parish church in the white community was hardly the scene of much action during the heyday of the civil rights movement. Nor is it the scene of much action today in the area of politics and law. But in terms of the basic illness afflicting our nation—in terms of the real root of our problem—I would submit that the parish church is *where the action is*—or ought to be—if we are ever going to cure this illness or solve this problem. For this is where the people are. This is where we deal with human beings, not abstractions of law and politics. This is where human beings are either lost or saved, damned or redeemed; and this is where the real issue will either be won or lost.

It is understandable that many an "activist" Christian—and I include myself in this category, emotionally, if not effectively—is often tempted to write off or close up the thousands of "First Churches" up and down this land of ours because of their seeming irrelevance and impotence. But to do so would be not only to reject these millions whom our Lord loves every bit as much as he does the activist, but also to make a strategic and tactical error of the first magnitude. For it is in these thousands of local congregations across the land that the struggle for the reconciliation of man to God and man to man is going to be won or lost.

In the arena of politics, as in the Western movie, the line is inevitably drawn between the "good guys" and the "bad guys," and the distinctions are relatively easy to make. Furthermore, since there is so little real communication between the two, the image of each remains rather rigidly fixed in the minds of both. But when we deal with real people, caught up in the common perplexities, joys, and sorrows of this life, the distinctions begin to blur, and we tend to see different degrees of *need*, rather than different degrees of evil. I have seen many a "redneck" racist in my day, and, with the exception of a few psychotics, I know of none whose basic affliction could not be cured by the same things that I require for my own soul's health: love and acceptance, mercy and forgiveness, compassion and grace.

The church is in business to mediate these things to the children of men; and most of these children are going to be reached, if at all, through the parish church. Not because the parish church is the only instrument for this work, and not because it is necessarily the best—but simply because this is where most of the children *are!*

This doesn't mean that the parish church can go on being just what it has been all these years—especially the *white* parish church. God forbid! Changes, already long overdue, have to be made: and, by God's grace, they *can* be made, *if* we don't give up on the people and treat them with condescension and contempt. And whatever specific forms these changes take, three underlying principles are essential.

First, there must be regular and meaningful confrontation with the issues at stake. Put another way, I suppose this means that we must constantly hear and proclaim God's word of judgment on our society and ourselves. Obviously, there has been all too little of this in our local congregations. Indeed, we have become masters of the art of evasion and distraction. We have wasted our time, energy, and resources in building programs, bazaars, and banalities. And all too often when God's word of judgment *has* been spoken, it has been in harsh, self-righteous terms that make too neat a distinction between the "good guy" (me) and the "bad guy" (you), when in reality it is "we" who are in this thing together.

The average white church member confronts the issue of race time and time again outside the church; but there he can deal with it in terms of law, economics, and custom, if he is so disposed. But within the parish church he must wrestle with it on the level of conscience, morality, and religion; and he is done a grave injustice if he is not regularly given the opportunity to do so. His mind and heart may not change, but he must have the opportunity to wrestle and to struggle with the real issue for the sake of his own soul.

Secondly, there must be provided by the parish opportunities for experience and channels for service that relate to this basic problem that we face. And here we must be concerned both with the congregation as a whole and with individual members of that congregation, realizing that the congregation as a whole will never move or grow as fast as some of its members. For example, one white Mississippi parish that I know wrestled long and hard with the matter of housing a Head Start center in its parish house, coming up in the end with an answer in the negative. But some two dozen members of that same parish were moved to launch a year-round program of volunteer service in the existing Head Start centers so that they as individuals could express their concern. At the same time, the parish itself did undertake the construction and maintenance of a low-rent housing project for poverty-level families—a project which would involve all members of the congregation. The parish as a whole could move on one level, while individuals could participate on another, but all received the stimulus from the local church.

In view of the crisis we face today, such an example may seem like pouring cups of water on a forest fire. But we must remember that growth, understanding, and a measure of reconciliation do come from such personal experience and contact, and, also, that these people belong to the overwhelming majority who will never be marching in the streets, but who are, in the final analysis, the real key to the ultimate resolution of our problems.

Finally, though, the parish church must somehow communicate the gospel of Jesus Christ. And I mean the *real* gospel; the good news that God loves me, accepts me, and forgives me, where I am and as I am—and that he does this for everyone else also! The good news that he has

made me a member of a family the whole world big and
that my human brothers and sisters and I are already *one*
in Jesus Christ; that God has reconciled us to himself and
to the rest of this family in Jesus Christ, and that we are
already members one of another. When I can once get
this through my thick skull and into my anxious heart, I
can stop worrying about human differences; I can stop
worrying about status, position, and power, and start
worrying about what I am doing to my fellow man by
failing to *act* like one whom God has reconciled to
himself.

A few folks seem to have gotten the message, God
bless 'em; but the rest of us still have a long way to go.
The only real point I would make in this brief sketch is
that most of "the rest of us" are to be found *in the parish
church;* and if we are ever going to be reached, it's going
to be there. That's where the action is—or where it should
be—because that's where the people are!

PART 3

11

Sick and Tired of Being Sick and Tired

FANNIE LOU HAMER

I am often asked, "What is the future of black people in America?" This is a very important question for any political campaign. I think the answer to it will explain *why* black people in Mississippi are going to vote, and *who* they are going to vote for. For what happens about politics in the next few years will have much to do with the future of black people in America. And that means that politics will have much to do with the future of all Americans, for we are in this thing together, white and black, yellow and red, brown and polka dot.

Some people say that we have counted too much on politics to cure America's racism, and to give black people what has been ours since white people began *integra-*

MRS. FANNIE LOU HAMER is a leader in the freedom movement in her native Mississippi and in the United States. She is a founder and vice-chairman of the Mississippi Freedom Democratic Party. She traveled to Europe and Africa in 1965 on behalf of several civil rights organizations. Mrs. Hamer lives in Ruleville, Mississippi, and speaks throughout the United States for the impoverished and rejected of our society. She is a member of the Board of the Committee of Southern Churchmen.

tion over three hundred years ago when they unloaded the first slave ships on the Atlantic coast. (They didn't bring *segregation* until about ninety years ago.) And sometimes there does seem to be something about America's politics that can't deal with the problems of what the white man is doing to the black man and the red man and the Mexican-American and the Puerto Rican and other minorities. I want to say something about that later on. But black people in the South in the past ten or fifteen years have spent so much time in politics—in voter registrations, in elections, in trying to work in political parties to influence them—that it does not seem to me that we can turn our backs completely on politics, as bad as it seems today.

We can still use politics to try to make America face the truth about its sickness, its racism, for the truth is the only thing that is going to free all of us in America today. After what happened in Chicago in 1968, I do think that black people and white people have got to work harder at politics at the grass roots. This is as important for poor white people as it is for black people; and it is important for any of the white people who say that they want a change in the way things are done in politics today. We have got to work harder at the grass roots. We have got to be careful that we don't lose what we have already gained there by what we do in future elections.

I believe that we have just got to keep some kind of faith that the people who want to make this country a good place to live can gain and influence politics in this country. I do have faith, as bad as the situation is now, for faith is the substance of things hoped for and the evidence of things not seen. If I hadn't had faith in 1964, I wouldn't have gone to Atlantic City, New Jersey, to tell the Democratic Convention why the Mississippi Freedom Democratic Party should be seated in place of the "regular" Democrats from Mississippi. And if I didn't have faith, I wouldn't keep pushing as hard as I am for what my people in the Freedom Democratic Party want. My people are saying that none of the candidates is spotless, but some of them are threatening to do things that would be a disaster to them and to the country, and that we must support the candidate who best relates to where we are right now. I have to have some kind of faith to keep up that kind of work. And if I didn't have faith, I wouldn't spend so much of my time talking to ninety percent white audiences all over the country and going to these ninety percent white political conventions.

I have been brutally beaten and permanently injured by white men while I was in jail for no other crime than trying to get citizens of Mississippi to register and vote. But I do not say that every white man in the country would do the same thing to me that a handful of white men did in Mississippi. And I do not say that everybody in the political arena in Chicago in 1968 was bad. There were some good people there. But we have a question to raise to America today, because America must wake up and learn the truth about itself and its racism. And that is one big thing that politics can do about racism in America today.

* * *

But we must begin by saying that the signs are not too hopeful that politics is going to help the black people a whole lot, at least not in the immediate future. Just think about the Kerner Commission report, as it spoke about the responsibility of "white racism" for the riots in the summer of 1967, and about the billions of dollars needed to deal with the ghettos. But this Report upset the President of the United States very much. So he did nothing about it. But he did sign the so-called "anti-crime bill," which contains many things directed against urban black people, and he got through an income tax hike to help pay for Vietnam. The Vice President of the United

States, Mr. Humphrey, publicly disagreed with the "white racism" part of the Kerner Commission's Report. And the Congress was not only hostile to the Report and to the Poor People's Campaign and to Resurrection City— less than two months after they seemed so sorry that Dr. King had been murdered—but everything they have done lately has shown that they are more interested in more profits and power for the rich and the powerful people, and they have no interest in helping the poor people, and they can still think up plenty of ways to embarrass poor people because they are poor.

Martin Luther King—soon after beginning a more directly political role—was murdered. Senator Robert Kennedy—soon after raising once again the hopes of poor minorities, black, red, Mexican-American, in his political campaign—was murdered, two months after Dr. King was murdered. Can anybody be surprised that we wonder if they were killed because America didn't want to have to face up to the truth? The two most effective political spokesmen for black people and minority groups were taken from us within two months, at the very time many of us believed was the best and probably the last chance for us to get some political success instead of being on the receiving end of the white racist politics which have dominated politics almost completely since our nation began.

You see, politics today is used by the white people not only to keep down the poor black and poor white and poor red man and others who are poor—for instance, the way Senator Eastland, the chairman of the Senate Judiciary Committee, does in my county, Sunflower County, Mississippi, and throughout America. Politics today is used by the white man to make the white man more wealthy and more powerful, just because he is already white, and wealthy and powerful—as President Johnson's Department of Agriculture did for Senator Eastland in my county, Sunflower County, Mississippi.

The Department of Agriculture gave Senator Eastland $157,930 in 1967 *not to plant crops* in the area of the county where black men and women and children were starving; and it also paid eight other plantation owners in Sunflower County more than $100,000 *each* last year not to grow crops. All that money going into my county would buy a lot of Food Stamps for the poor and hungry people, black and white, in Mississippi. But that same Agriculture Department that paid Senator Eastland and the other plantation owners so much money for *not* growing crops turns back millions of dollars to the Treasury Department that ought to be used for Food Stamps to feed these starving people. One reason they can turn back the money is because many times the Food Stamp programs are controlled by local and county governments that don't want poor people to have anything to eat, so that they will go away, maybe, to the ghettos and slums of Detroit and Chicago and Newark and New York City. Now some Congressmen and Washington officials are saying that there is no one starving in America. They are only getting "improper diets." But personally I can't see the difference. And I *know* the black children who are sick all the time and have bloated little bellies because of what they can't get to eat do not know the difference.

This is one of the things that politics—that is, white man's politics—means to black people, and one of the things we black people want to use politics to change. For this sort of thing just isn't right. When you speak of "politics and racial progress" you are asking whether politics is going to help the black people and other people have their rightful share in the future of the good things that America has. But to ask *that* question is to say things do not look good for black people, and for all of America, today.

* * *

But I still have some hope. And to explain why, I think

I ought to go back and explain how I first became
involved in the struggle for freedom and human rights in
Mississippi in 1962, and draw the line of my own experiences forward to today. I am from Sunflower County,
Mississippi, from the most rural and the poorest area in
the USA. In Sunflower County, we have 38,000 blacks,
17,000 whites. We have 14,000 potential black voters,
8,000 potential white voters. In Sunflower County, we
have 150% of the white voters registered, but not quite
50% of the black voters registered. Now the reason I say
150% of the white voters are registered is because in my
county they vote who are dead and are not yet born.
Anyway, I shall never forget when I attended my first
mass meeting, in Ruleville, Mississippi, on the Monday
night after the fourth Sunday in August, 1962. The
Student Non-violent Coordinating Committee and the
Southern Christian Leadership Conference came into Mississippi in August 1962 to get black people to register to
vote. I went to their meeting in Ruleville, where the
Reverend James Bevel preached a sermon from Matthew
16:3—"discerning the signs of the times"—tying it to
voter registration. Then Jim Foreman talked about how it
was our constitutional right as citizens to register and to
vote in Mississippi.

That night they asked us to go down the following
Friday, and I agreed to try for the first time in my life to
register to vote. On Friday, eighteen of us went to Indianola, the county seat, in an old bus that a Negro man
used in the summer to haul cotton-choppers and cotton-
pickers, and in the winter to take many of the same
people to Florida to work in the fields there, because
there wasn't enough work in Mississippi to keep food on
their tables. We went to the clerk's office in the courthouse, and he asked us what we wanted there. I told him
we had come to try to register. Then he said, "Well, all of
you will have to leave this room except *two.*" I was one
of the two persons he let stay in his office to take what

he called the "literacy test." Now this "literacy test"
consisted of twenty-one questions. It began: "What is
your full name?" "Write the date of this application."
Then it went on to questions such as: "By whom are you
employed?"—this meant that you would be fired by the
time you got back home. "Where is your place of resi-
dence in this district?"—this meant that the Ku Klux
Klan and the White Citizen's Council would be given your
address. It asked: "If there is more than one person of
the same name in this precinct, by what name do you
want to be called?" After we answered that kind of
question, the clerk pointed out a section of the Mississippi Constitution, told us to copy it and then give a
reasonable interpretation of it—and that was the first
time, in August 1962, that I knew that Mississippi had a
constitution! It was a hard thing to do, to stay around
there in that courthouse and work on that "literacy test."
It took the eighteen of us until about 4:30 in the afternoon to finish it, and it was a hard thing to do, to stay in
that courthouse all day long. People came in and out of
the courthouse with cowboy boots on, and with rifles
and with dogs.

But we finally did finish this "literacy test" and started
back for home. About two miles out of Indianola, some
lawmen stopped us and ordered us all off the bus. We got
off, then they told us to get back on. When we did, they
carried us back to Indianola, and fined the bus driver
$100 for driving a bus painted the wrong color. They said
that there was *too much yellow* on the bus that day. They
finally agreed to lower the fine to $30, which the eigh-
teen of us made up to pay so we could return to Ruleville. I went back to my home in the rural area, on the
land of a man I'd worked for as a sharecropper and
timekeeper for eighteen years. As I came up to my house,
my oldest daughter and her little cousin came out to
meet me, and told me that the man I worked for was
blazing mad because I had gone down and tried to regis-

ter. When I got home my husband told me the same thing. Then, the landowner came and called my husband out of the house and asked him if I had "made it back." He said I had, and then I walked out on the porch, and the owner said, "Did Pap tell you what I said?" And I said, "Yes, sir (because this was still the pattern in the South in August 1962. It's only been in the last two or three years that this old pattern has been broken, although a lot of black people still say "yes, sir" and "no, sir" to a white man, no matter who he is, or how old he is). Anyway, the landowner said to me, "You'll have to go back down there and withdraw that thing, or you'll have to leave." And I told him, "I didn't go down there to register for you, I went down there to register for myself." I had to leave my home that night, the 31st of August, 1962. Then ten days later, sixteen bullets were fired into the home of Mr. and Mrs. Robert Tucker, the people I was staying with in Ruleville after I had to leave my home. And that same night, two Negro girls were shot.

This has been the pattern of harassment we have had in Mississippi simply because we participated in voter registration work and in politics. For example, early in 1963, there was a knock on our door, and when my husband opened it, a policeman came in just to intimidate us. But this sort of thing didn't stop my work in the voter registration in Mississippi. Then on June 9, 1963, I was arrested in Winona, Mississippi, USA, and while I was in jail there I was beaten so badly that one of my kidneys was permanently damaged and I received a bloodclot that almost caused me to lose the sight of my left eye. But we kept at our work, for we knew that we had to have a change, not only for the blacks in Mississippi but for the poor whites as well. We tried very hard to work with the so-called "regular" Democratic party in Mississippi, first by going to work on the precinct level. But that didn't work. When I went to a precinct meeting in Ruleville, my husband, who had just been hired on a new job, was fired from that job the next day.

After failures of that sort, we were convinced that they were not going to let us get into their "regular" Democratic Party in Mississippi. That was when we organized what is called the Mississippi Freedom Democratic Party, at the Masonic Temple in Jackson, Mississippi, in June 1964. I was elected vice-chairman of the delegation that went to the Democratic National Convention in Atlantic City in August 1964 to challenge the seating of the "regular" Democrats from Mississippi. Mr. Ed King, a white native-born of Mississippi, was elected chairman. That was the time when we found out what *national* politics was like. That was the time when we found out that politics in the United States was the same as politics in Mississippi. I saw and heard people threatening us, and threatening those who took a stand with us in the Mississippi Freedom Democratic Party. I have been told that President Johnson himself decided to hold a "news conference" to be put on television in order to take the television cameras away from me when I was testifying before the Credentials Committee of the Democratic National Convention. It was when I was telling about the beatings I received in jail. So the truth we were trying to tell about politics must have been making it hot for even the highest leaders of the Democratic Party.

Another meeting I shall never forget was with Hubert Humphrey before he was nominated for Vice President. Mr. Joseph Rauh, Jr., of the Americans for Democratic Action, told us at that meeting that if we didn't "cool off" what we were doing, if we didn't stop pressing to take our fight to the floor of the Convention, Senator Humphrey wouldn't be nominated that night for Vice President of the United States. Mr. Humphrey was sitting right there with tears in his eyes, when Mr. Rauh of the ADA was talking like that to us. So I asked: "Is Mr. Humphrey's position more important to him than

400,000 black people who live in Mississippi?" They didn't answer me, but after I asked that question, I wasn't permitted in the meetings with the Democratic leaders any more. We were told that we should accept a "compromise": two at-large votes in the Convention. But we refused to accept a "compromise." We argued that if something was supposed to be ours three hundred years ago, no one has the right to hand us only a *part* of it now. We argued that we wanted *every bit* of what was ours, and that we wanted it *now*. We argued that we were not ever going to get what was ours by taking a bit now, and a bit later, because that would make us forget what it was we had the full right to have!

So we didn't accept a compromise, and we went back home to Mississippi. In Knoxville, Tennessee, we were stopped by the Ku Klux Klan, and it took five cars of patrolmen to guard us from Knoxville to Chattanooga. After we got back to Mississippi we tried unsuccessfully to get on the ballots to run as candidates. So we made up our own ballots with the same candidates as on the regular ballot, only with my name added to run in the Second Congressional District against Jamie Whitten. I received 33,009 votes and Jamie Whitten got only 49 votes. (That was when they saw the political power that black people had in the Second Congressional District in Mississippi: one night I went to bed, and didn't turn over and didn't move, but when I woke up, I woke up in the First Congressional District, which is where I am now.) Mr. King and some of us went to Washington, D.C., on January 4, 1965, to challenge the seating of the five "regular" Democratic representatives from Mississippi. We wanted a study made of the elections, we wanted depositions and evidence taken so that they could see who really deserved to be seated from Mississippi.

They didn't dismiss our challenge at that time. So we asked lawyers to come to Mississippi—over one hundred came—to collect evidence. We were able to get three volumes of evidence—15,000 pages—proving why the five white representatives should not be seated in Congress. But on September 13, 1965, we received a telegram from the Speaker of the House, Mr. John McCormack, saying that they wanted to have a hearing to discuss the dismissal—not of the representatives, but of our *challenge!* So we went to Washington, D.C., again to appear before the Subcommittee on Elections, and the way we were treated that time wasn't any different from the way we had been treated in Mississippi or in Atlantic City. The hearing was closed to the public. At the hearing what they were saying was: "We won't say you Negroes are not right, but if we let *you* get away with it, they'll be doing the same thing all over the South." So on September 17, 1965, Congressmen William Fitts Ryan and Don Edwards and some others escorted us into the gallery of the House of Representatives until they called for the challenge to come to the floor of the House. When they called for it, we went out of the gallery and down to the floor while they argued and then dismissed our challenge.

* * *

Racial progress? Almost a hundred years ago, John R. Lynch placed this same kind of challenge before the House of Representatives. He was a black man from Mississippi, and he succeeded with Yankee white help. But we failed a hundred years later with native white Mississippi help and Yankee opposition. We had all kinds of evidence to prove that these five men should not be seated in the House, starting from the fact that Mississippi was readmitted to the Union in 1870 after agreeing and signing a pledge that they would not disenfranchise any citizens, black or white. In 1972, the five white men from Mississippi still sit in the House of Representatives, but they took the seat away from Adam Clayton Powell, a black man. What America must do is see what is happening: they didn't unseat Powell, they unseated *us*, the black people. And they only "censured" Senator Thomas Dodd, they did not unseat him; they gave him a pat on the back and go-ahead, telling him just don't get caught. So you see, this is not Mississippi's problem, it is America's problem.

All of it is America's problem. Many, many of the threatening letters and telegrams I've received since I was on television in Atlantic City weren't from Mississippi. I've had telegrams from Chicago and other places in the North telling me what we shouldn't have done and what ought to happen to us. In Atlantic City I got a letter with a picture of a heart and a dagger through the heart, and reading under it, telling me to go back to Africa. So since that time, whenever I've spoken to an audience with white people in it, I've hoped that the person who sent that message is there, so he can hear my answer to his message. I'd like to tell him, we'll make a deal: after they've sent all the Australians back to Australia, and the Koreans back to Korea, and the Chinese back to China, and the Italians back to Italy, and the Germans back to Germany, and then give the Indians back their land, and then get on the Mayflower from whence they came . . . then, *we* will go home too.

A little poem from *Freedom Ways* magazine sums up the way most white politicians have acted toward us:

> *This is a story of folks black like me—*
> *No longer slaves but not yet free.*
> *Told what they can do,*
> *And told what they shan't.*
> *Told what do do,*
> *And told what to don't.*
> *Damned if we do, and damned if we don't.*

Now this has been the pattern, not only in Mississippi, not only in the South, but through America. We black people are caught in so many petty ways. One of the questions that always comes up in an integrated meeting on "race relations" is to tell the Negroes: *"What about education?" "Give education a chance!"* You tell *us, we* should integrate the schools! We get three black children in your schools, and you start complaining about *that.* My little daughter is the product of what is called by the white people an "integrated" school. And the suffering that kid is going through . . . why, I wouldn't put her in there to go through that for another year for anything. But then, when I take her out, you'll say we've segregated ourselves. Yes, you are right, we need education. And we're going to educate our kids, *somehow.* But white Americans are going to have to deal with black Americans *while our kids are getting this education.* Black people are fed up and sick and tired of white people saying that "we can't stand to hear all this talk about integration." White Americans, *you* started it when you unloaded the ships of black people in your slave ships from Africa. And *you* started that other kind of "integration" you claim you are so scared about: I have cousins as white as any white man or woman in America. They have blue eyes and yellow hair, and I know a black man didn't do *that.* It's time for America to face up to the reality of this matter. You have got to get done with this scapegoat about your son marrying my daughter. We couldn't care less about that. But we do want to be treated as human beings.

One thing I always think about when I hear all this talk about the trouble we black people are causing by demanding integration is a letter I received from one of my friends some months ago. He was told by the State Department or Defense Department or someone that his son would soon be home from Vietnam. And the letter went on to say that "if your son jumps up when he hears a telephone ring, and runs out into the street or into the back yard and starts digging a foxhole, just have patience with him. And if your son takes his gravy and pours it on his dessert, just bear with him a little longer." There were some other things that that letter said—I couldn't understand all the language—but they just told my friend to have faith and to be patient with their son, and he *might* speak English again.

This is the product of Vietnam. This is why black Americans are so tired that now they are sick and tired of *being sick and tired*. We are sick and tired of our people having to go to Vietnam and other places to fight for something we don't have here, and then come home with such letters as this. What we want to do is to make this a better country, to end the wrongs such as fighting a war in Vietnam and pouring billions over there, while people in Sunflower County, Mississippi, and Harlem and Detroit are starving to death because of something that is not their fault. I know, a lot of people say that our people are sorry, that we don't work or won't do anything, because if we would, we'd not be in the shape we're in now, needing education and everything. But just remember, when the power structure had me and *my* kids and *my* people in the cotton fields, they had *their* people in school. It took us a while to realize what was happening to us, but when we did, the cottonpicker caught up with the sack. And we're not going to give up now. We're going to move on up.

* * *

Now I want to say a word or two about the churches and this race situation. I travel quite a bit across this country, and a lot of the kids are asking, "Is God alive, or is he dead?" Now they *mean* it when they ask that question. They're not just trying to be smart or something like that. And I think I know what makes them ask that question: it is the hypocrites, the black and the white hypocrites, who make them ask that question. The hypocrites who do too much pretending and not enough actual working, the white ministers and the black ministers standing behind a podium and preaching a lie on Sunday. For what the kids are now asking is something like this: "If this is Christianity that is being offered in most of the churches around this land, then we don't want any part of it. Look at what is happening all over the land, and the churches don't seem to pay any attention to it." We have almost driven our young people from God with this big act of hypocrisy. We have to take them seriously—I know I do—when they say that God is not God if he lets all these huge churches pour millions of dollars into buildings for their own people, and let the kids in their own neighborhood go without food and without clothing and without decent shelter.

Everybody knows that the most segregated hour in America is the eleven o'clock church service. But there is something worse than that. That is when you see these white and black hypocrites in all of their fine clothes come out of a worship service, and turn up their nose at a kid in rags, or a man drunk on the street, and ask themselves, "Now what's wrong with *him?*" They never ask, "*Why* is that kid in rags?" "*Why* is that man drunk?" They never stop to think that it was something that put that kid in rags, just as it was something that drove that man to drink.

Just as it's time for America to wake up, it is long *past* time for the churches to wake up. The churches have got to say that they will have no more talk that "because your skin is a little different, you're better than they are." The churches have got to remember how Christ dealt with the poor people. He said, "The spirit of the Lord is upon me, because he hath anointed me to preach the gospel to the poor; he hath sent me to heal the brokenhearted, to preach deliverance to the captives, and recovering of sight to the blind, to set at liberty them that are bruised" (Luke 4:18). Jesus wasn't just talking about black people, or about white people, he was talking about *people*. There's no difference in people, for Paul says, "God hath made of one blood all nations of men for to dwell on all the face of the earth" (Acts 17:26). That means that whether we're white, black, red, yellow or polka dot, we're made from the same blood.

If Christ were here today, he would be branded a radical, a militant, and would probably be branded as "red." They have even painted *me* as Communist, although I wouldn't know a Communist if I saw one. A few weeks ago the FBI was checking on me, and the agent was telling me all the bad things the Communists would do. I told him, "Well, that *is* something! We've sure got a *lot* of Communists right up there in Washington, don't we, Ed?"

We have to realize just how grave the problem is in the United States today, and I think Ephesians 6:11 and 12 helps us to know how grave the problem is, and what it is we are up against: "Put on the whole armor of God, that ye may be able to stand against the wiles of the devil. For we wrestle not against flesh and blood, but against principalities, against powers, against the rulers of the darkness of this world, against spiritual wickedness in high places." This is what I think about when I think of my own work in the fight for freedom, because before 1962 I would have been afraid to have spoken before more than six people. Since that time I have had to speak before thousands in the fight for freedom, and I believe that God gave me the strength to be able to speak in this cause.

So we are faced with a problem that is not flesh and blood, but we are facing principalities and powers and spiritual wickedness in high places: that's what St. Paul told us. And that's what he meant. America created this problem. And we forgive America, even though we were brought here on the slave ships from Africa. Even though the dignity was taken away from the black men, and even though the black women had to bear not only their own kids but kids of the white slave owners. We forgive

America for that. But we're looking for this check now, that's long past due, to let us have our share in political and economic power, so that we can have a great country, together.

* * *

It's time for black people to stop being brainwashed with the idea that nobody can be right in this country except Mr. Charlie. Mr. Charlie's days are numbered, anyway. Black people have got to learn that it is time for them to stand up and be counted, because they are as much as anybody else. Black people have got to stop trying to be white. For if we live four hundred years, when we wake up we're still going to be black. We have to know this, and go on from there.

Black people have got to wake up.

Dr. King is dead.

It does not make sense now to stage demonstrations and mass marches and sit-ins and all the rest. At least, not the way we have done during the last ten years. The reason is that we have reached the point where it doesn't make sense any more to *ask* the government for anything by mass protests. We are not going to get *anything* that way. They are not going to give anything to black people any more just because black people ask for it, demonstrate for it. It seems to me that the question John Lewis asked at the March on Washington in 1963 is the question that has to be asked today: "Just what side is the federal government on?" For as hard as this may seem, the time has come now when we are going to have to get what we need for ourselves. We may get a little bit of help, here and there, but in the main, we are going to have to do for ourselves. If what the politicians have done to the poverty program hasn't taught us anything else, it has taught us that we are not going to get much help from the politicians. And it has taught us that we are not going to get any serious useful help from the government, to deal with problems we have because we are poor and because we are black.

But I don't think that means we can give up our work in politics. We have got to get something from politics, for politics owes us something. I know that some black people and white people are saying that we ought not to vote because the choices are so bad, and elections are not something that is important to black people anyway. But a lot of people, especially in the North, haven't gone through some of the terrible, almost unbearable things we have had to go through in the South. A lot of them who say they aren't going to vote really do not know what it is like to go hungry, and to know that thousands of people who get little or nothing from the govern-ment—welfare or food or anything—are starving to death. A lot of these folk don't know what we in the South know—of what it is like to work for twenty-five or thirty cents a day. By having this experience in the South, and by having gone through what I have just talked about—of what it meant a few years ago to register and vote in Mississippi—you can be sure that we will turn out and vote, and we are going to carry carloads of people to the polls.

It is time for America to wake up and realize that black Americans are not going to tolerate what we've had to put up with in the past three hundred years. We're *not* going to say that no more black people are going to die. I'm never sure anymore when I leave home whether I'll get back or not. Sometimes it seems like to tell the truth today is to run the risk of being killed. But if I fall, I'll fall five feet four inches forward in the fight for freedom. I'm not backing off that, and no one will have to cover the ground I walk on as far as freedom is concerned. No man is an island to himself, and until I'm free in Mississip-pi, you're not free anywhere else. A nation that's divided is definitely on the way out. We have the same problems from coast to coast.

The future for black people in America is the same as the future for white people in America. Our chances are the same. If you survive, we will too. If we crumble, you are going to crumble too.

So let each of us ask himself the question in the old hymn:

> *Must I be carried to the sky on flowery beds of ease,*
> *While others fight to win the prize and sail through*
> * bloody seas?*

12

Violence and Snopes

JAMES Y. HOLLOWAY

Detroit, Newark, Milwaukee, Washington—cities afire and simmering, while others have been spared. Is it too hasty or unduly pessimistic to offer the judgment that once again we have learned *nothing?*

Have we learned nothing because we have passed the point when we can be made to know in our hearts that something is dreadfully, perhaps fatally, wrong with us? That is, do our sins "not permit us to return to God" (Hosea 5:4)?

Without exception we react to our civil warfare by reflexes, with hollow gestures. A commission is appointed whose color and composition suggest a magisterial and cynical thumb of the nose by our highest elected official. With strained grief the chief executive of "the most powerful nation in history" spends two billion dollars a month to save freedom in Asia by killing the Asians. With the same gesture, he commissions a jury of blue ribbons

JAMES Y. HOLLOWAY is editor of *Katallagete* and teaches at Berea College, Kentucky. He is the editor of *Introducing Jacques Ellul* and, with Will D. Campbell, of *Up to Our Steeples in Politics.*

and silk stockings to exchange views on the fate of the victims of three hundred years of violence and racism. A visit and a two-hour talk *to any black* in the ghettos of the capital of "the most powerful nation in history," or in East Harlem, Newark, or Detroit, or in the 'cropper's cabins in south Alabama or Georgia or the Mississippi or Louisiana Delta would have told him all anyone needed to know. And the Congress of this "most powerful nation in history," with a few demurrers, shares this sense of value, priority, and political judgment.

And so does the nation. Speeches and editorials and cocktail lounge chatter call for more imaginative use of (*or* outright abolition of—there is really little difference in the two viewpoints) the Job Corps, the poverty program, black militancy, Sargent Shriver, tear gas, Teddy Kennedy, Spiro Agnew, and H. Rap Brown. It is all as cut-and-dried and now as much a part of our system as the war bulletins from Saigon or a statement by the President or Secretary of State or General Westmoreland or General Abrams or Tom Hayden on American aims in Southeast Asia.

This reflex response that is now built into our domestic war front should convince even the most determined optimist that government and politics are unable of themselves to reverse the direction of this nation's racism. Indeed, the contrary is true: our government and politics have for the most part aggravated racism since 1789 or 1865. To say—as do the political theorists of the death of God and the mainline sentiment of the New Politics and the ADA—that "if politics cannot solve our problems then they will not be solved" is simply to state the case and measure the depth of our tragedy. The sentiment does not change the realities about the direction in which politics and government are taking American racism.

Let us be clear about where we are, and about how we got here. From the very beginning, political involvement in America's racism—national, state, local, Republican,

Democrat—when it has not been the instrumentality to preserve white superiority, has, without exception, been skittish, giving half-hearted responses to the revolts and explosions of the black community. Politics has involved itself in American racism not because of a sense of injustice, but because blacks reacted with increasing vigor against the miserable and hopeless lot into which America's democracy had cast them. Black indignation and revolt against the politics of American democracy provoked whatever interest politics and government have devoted to ameliorating the most horrifying features of America's racism. Not a sense of injustice, but a sense of frustration, has been the characteristic attitude of American politics toward racial misery and unrest. It was inevitable, therefore, that political frustration would lead us to these present days of blasphemy.

There is, therefore, no sign, no hint—anywhere—that government and politics are capable of redirecting our national life in a way that can end, or even significantly modify, white racism. Government and politics in the twentieth century have become dominated by (and therefore obsessed with) the exercise of armed power to meet all problems that seem to threaten the existing social order. Two *world* wars, the increasing ratio of noncombatant deaths from 1914-1918 to Korea and Vietnam, the hydrogen and napalm apocalypse, Sheriffs Clark and Rainey, the riot police and National Guard, the 3800 .50-caliber holes in one wall in Detroit and the slaughter of Black Panthers Fred Hampton and Mike Clark in Chicago, together with the use of the "law" to hide the truth—all these are cases in point. Government and politics have become the exercise of those instrumentalities that delude themselves and their citizenry into thinking that they can solve political and social crises by destroying the bodies of their political and social opponents. Other functions—social security, health insurance, employment, education, etc.—now devolve from this function. Check any budget of the United States since 1940. List those political and social crises that have been "solved"—in the sense of eliminated—by the use of physical force.

Consequently, the most legitimate action government and politics could exercise against racism in America would be self-restraint, a limitation of their own use of physical coercion. But if they did so—we will ask and be asked—how can government be "responsible"? How can it meet its commitments and honor its pledges of law and order here and abroad? How can our shops and streets and investments be made safe if politics and government restrain rather than escalate their use of force? No right-thinking citizen can demand the restraint of the police and National Guard or ask General Abrams to tie his hands in Southeast Asia. Of course not. The whole direction of our government and politics through the escalation of force in social crises aggravates the situation it seeks to overcome. Democrat, Republican, New Politics and Birchite are simply four identical ways of looking at the same blackbird.

In a word, the violence employed by government and politics to meet the crises of white racism in America incites counterviolence in the victims of this violence. This antiphony of violence by political authority and counterviolence by oppressed blacks, which describes the present state of racism in America today, bids fair to become the obsession that may divert the nation from whatever chance there remains to amend this racism. There is, for example, ample evidence suggesting that the study of violence and its "morality" is the next detour that intellectuals and theologians will travel. Insofar as Christians are concerned, it is necessary to recall our own witness to and about violence. By and large, since the third century, we have celebrated it, made a cult of it, because we Christians have exercised the preponderance of such violence in Western culture. But when violence occasionally threatens our property (and incidentally our lives) we condemn it—in *all* forms. Today, to retain full membership in the Crisis-of-the-Month Club, there is every prospect that our theologians will begin to inquire into the "anatomy of violence" and to write papers and conduct seminars on "theology and violence," or even the "theology *of* violence." We may expect to be instructed in the linguistic distinctions in the Old and New Testaments between "to kill" and "to murder," just as we have been told about alleged distinctions between "just" and "unjust" wars.

But like most detours of the great god Relevance, it is in reality a dead end. The question of violence is not clarified by "anatomies" of violence, theologies of violence, or etymologies of "to murder" and "to kill." Moreover, all this pandering to the god Relevance can neither mitigate nor direct racial violence, any more than it can tell us anything really "new" about violence. Racial violence is at this moment beyond the powers of anyone or anything—the President, Rap Brown, the National Guard, RAM, and tear gas—to control or direct. The fact is that it is now pointless to ask how we can avoid violence. The only questions now are: How *much* violence will there be, and what *form* and *direction* will it take? Nonetheless, the rat control bill, attacks on the poverty program, the decision to build an ABM system, bailing out Lockheed Aircraft, the passion for riot control bills in the Congress and the states, the determination to spend three billion dollars a month in Vietnam if necessary, the training of the National Guard for duty as domestic police, and compacts between the states to trade off these troops—all this portends that the principal course government and politics will continue to pursue to "solve" racism is a violent one—that is, the employment of all the men necessary and all the techniques of modern warfare available to suppress and contain the resistance of black people to the American ghetto of squalor, despair, inhumanity, and hopelessness.

Any Christian witness against violence must begin, therefore, where it left off eighteen, and maybe twenty, centuries ago: a witness against *any* use of violence to solve political and social problems that would destroy the lives of political and social opponents. Politics is means, not Messiah, because life is more—indeed, other—than politics. Should the intellectuals (accepting the faggots thrown in by the theologians) offer an ideology of violence to the black community of America, and should the black community accept it, the "final solution" of the "black problem" would be provided by the honkies. To think that violence can redirect the white community's racism into the brotherhood of man is to capitulate before the ideology of the honkies, and in the end to become a honky. To think that violence can redirect enmity into brotherhood is to ignore the most obvious "lesson" of Vietnam. But to say this, to plead that violence cannot alter America's racism, is not a message of "nonviolence" from the Christian community (largely white and middle class) to the black community (largely impoverished and oppressed); it is rather a message to the government and politics of our nation (largely white and middle class) to desist from launching an attempt to solve this nation's racial crises by violence.

* * *

An even greater danger in the obsession with violence is the faith that racial violence will somehow become organized, widespread, effectively destroy meaningful property (and probably lives) and paralyze a large segment of American society, so that "something" will *have* to be done. But the evidence so far is heavily against it, especially against the faith that the "something" will be conciliatory. The evidence so far is that *if* a segment of America were somehow paralyzed by a violent uprising, the "something" that followed would be so oppressive and complete as to commit this nation irrevocably to a proud—and legalized—apartheid police state.

Is this sort of overt violence the final direction our racism is apt to take? Does not the evidence so far suggest the contrary? Instead of the great conflagration inciting "something" to be done, is not another pattern already discernible? Watts—and pacification by police, Marines, and the National Guard. Pause. Next, Newark and Detroit, and pacification by police and National Guard. Pause. After perhaps six months, or nine months, Cleveland and San Francisco, and more pacification. Pause. Next, Milwaukee and Jacksonville, or perhaps Columbia, South Carolina, or maybe Waycross, Georgia, and more pacification. Pause. And so on, with each uprising like the preceding one, capricious, irrational, small-scale, without plans or strategies relating one action to another, and unorganized in its initiation and early phase. A city or two one week—repression, pause, nothing noticeably altered anywhere except in the devastation of the pacified area, which is, relatively speaking, small and insignificant. Then three months later, two towns and a large city—repression, pause, nothing noticeably altered anywhere. Perhaps a leader is killed and another disappears, but nothing noticeable. There's plenty of color TV, plenty of bombs on Vietnam, plenty of strikes, plenty of debates over taxes, but nothing is noticeably altered anywhere.

But each repression becomes more efficient because the technicians in the police control points have all the apparatus to heighten and perfect the repression—in a word, to make the repression technically more efficient and the pause less noticeable, more normal. Justice? It's identical with the law that upholds *our* (white) order and protects *our* property and ensures the safety of *our*

streets. (After all, *that* was the real issue in 1968.) Plans
have already been discussed at governors' conferences
about exchanging units of the National Guard: Memphis
is closer to Little Rock than to Nashville; Philadelphia is
closer to New York than to Pittsburgh. Regionalism will
work under the right kinds of pressure. Moreover, a
malicious chief executive could always have the telegraph lines tied up in order to spotlight a governor's
inability to deal forcefully with a crisis.

From the Pentagon to the sheriff's office in Neshoba
County, the technicians have all the apparatus to rationalize racial uprisings by black citizens. It has to do with
the technical mentality of the American people, with the
technical efficiency of the police, with cybernation, with
self-correcting mechanisms, as each uprising feeds information about itself into the machine. The machine learns,
remembers (in a way humans will not), and knows what
and how to do better "next time," and the public is
satisfied because it is not personally or materially incon-
venienced. To expect the great conflagration to get us out
of our racism, or in the twentieth century to expect a
genuine crisis to catapult us violently into the police state
is to indulge in fantasy. Rather, we will be--or, more
accurately, are being—computerized into the technological police state *at our own doing:* it is the only way law
and order today can protect the property and maintain
the order of the white establishment.

Hence—in contrast to the great conflagration producing a dramatic "something" that redeems or damns—we
shall be denied the advantage of being surprised one gray
morning to wake up and find ourselves in the concentration camp of the technological era. The chief characteristic of the technological police state is that it is our own
doing, our own work, our own achievement, our "Final
Solution"—that, and the absence of any overt, dramatic
event or sign that we, blithely oblivious to the fact, are

being eased into the technological concentration camp. Not Auschwitz, not Dachau, but the Secular City: convenience, order and respectability.

In everything that has happened between Watts and Detroit, this pattern is more obvious than the pattern suggesting the great conflagration into "something." We ignore it at our peril. Police methods and the use of violence by government and politics have become so rationalized and effective in advanced industrial-technological societies that it is difficult to envision a genuine crisis—that is, an overt and violent event that forces a change in either direction—by conflagration. After all, the charge that the "authorities" leveled most often against the police and National Guard operations in Newark and Detroit was inefficiency, not injustice and brutality. The brave new world, the Secular City of 1984, will not result from a gigantic and damning crisis provoking us to this eventuality, for such a crisis might conceivably force a reversal of the direction of our racism. The real "crisis" of the technological era is *that there is no crisis,* no conflagration and violence to provoke "something."

* * *

Perhaps William Faulkner's saga of Flem and the other Snopeses is the most accurate vision yet of the technological era—a vision that begins, lest we forget, with the "barn burning" (and the threats to burn barns) of Flem's daddy. (And perhaps this vision of Snopes stands in sharpest contradiction to Faulkner's own profession of faith that "man will prevail"—if that man is Flem Snopes, who is marked by what he wrought in his communities during his lifetime.)

For in the technological society Snopes is in charge. And the Snopes of Snopes is to seek respectability—not justice, not virtue, but respectability—and thereby to gain power and control and money. But the Snopes of Snopes is to seek respectability by *not* provoking a crisis by conflagration, by *not* burning a barn, by *not* committing murder—or by *not* being caught. To do otherwise—to fall into the failure of a crisis by conflagration, to get caught at barn burning—is to threaten the very respectability which the Snopes of the industrial-technological society must have to maintain himself and his order. Snopes and technique fail when they ignite or cannot rationalize a conflagration, a genuine crisis. But while Flem is murdered, what he is and what he did cannot be killed.

It was not the immorality but rather the inefficiency of Johnson's war policy in Vietnam that made possible the massing of significant dissent from mainstream America—including, especially, the dissent heard from the universities and the church. The explanation for this is simple: mainstream America had neither the tradition nor the perspective from which to criticize the "immorality" of the Vietnam war or *any* war. University and church were hostages to the political messianism of the twentieth century. What dissent there was (and is) could be mounted only when the quick resolution of the war did not follow from the fantastic tandem of escalation bombing and search-and-destroy missions—a policy which Johnson switched on, but which he did not conceive. In any event, following what they learned from the pattern of how to handle the "all deliberate speed" of fifteen years ago, the bureaucracy simply wore the agitation out. The bureaucracy had nowhere to go; the agitation did: ecology, women's liberation, etc., etc.

And what, after all, is the real horror of My Lai? Not the women and babies ripped apart by the most advanced weaponry of technology's arsenal in the hands of American boys carrying out America's policies. Not that. We have had plenty of that put before us by the scholars and newsmen and photographers reporting about our victims in North and South Vietnam, Korea, the Dominican

Republic, Tokyo, Hiroshima, and Nagasaki; any part of it would equal what was found in My Lai, with no official expressions of horror and no threats of courts-martial or even of a war crime tribunal. Not that. My Lai is the image of women and babies ripped apart at point-blank range, their eyes terrorized and incredible, staring into the eyes of their American executioners inches away. *That* is the horror of My Lai. Not the *victims* of our decisions. The victims of Hiroshima and Nagasaki and Hanoi and Saigon are just as grotesque, but Senators and Congressmen and citizens had no public complaints about those victims disturbing their stomach juices. The image of *how* it happened at My Lai—point-blank, American boys, terrorized eyes, mutilated babies—that is the image we cannot live with in the technological era. It is not the same image as bombers launched from the technological marvel of aircraft carriers, dispatched by radar, blessed by Christ's own. That is the image we can live with—the morally isolated image, two miles up from the ripped and bleeding victims, American boys staring not into their benumbed and pleading eyes inches away, but peering through oxygen-filled masks into the gadgets, dials, needles, buttons, switches and radar. That is clean, like our image of pastel-tiled bathrooms. We can live with that image. And that is what it means to live in the technological era. Snopes, like the Bible, teaches that the punishment fits the crime.

The Christian must learn to live in a technological concentration camp controlled by Snopes and his ideology of respectability, an integral part of said respectability being a member of the church as well as president of the bank. Any way "out" must begin, therefore, with an understanding of the nature of the victory of Snopes and technique. The victory of Snopes, as the victory of technique, is the achievement of results by indirection, by the use of science, by maneuver (which might also include "rumors" of barn burning), by calculation and reason guided by the values of efficiency and effectiveness and permeated with respectability, by seeing that the barricades are never stormed, by permitting only pseudo-crises, not real crises, and by the community accepting Snopes as "Mister" without thinking to ask itself: "When did we begin to call him Mister?"

* * *

Where is the Good News in all this? Where it has always been. God's death by violence on the cross and his victory in the resurrection were not the result of the triumph of our violence, of our provocation of a crisis or manipulation of a pseudo-crisis, but the victory of *his* Word. And this is just about all that can be said. Yes, there are signs to be discerned. The punishment fits the crime. The inevitable resort to violence to crush ghetto uprisings against the sins of centuries thrusts us, black and white, straightway into the technological concentration camp of contemporary society. The violence that has been part of the tradition and cult of our history, and which our academicians and theologians may yet raise into the cult of technological violence as have their brothers and cousins in government and politics, now renders any modification of white racism almost impossible. And the technology we created and worship, as the children of Israel created and worshiped the golden calf, will provide the "Final Solution" for both blacks and whites in America as we are computed at our own insistence into the society of Snopes.

But the Good News is still "here." Perhaps the only way we will ever discern the reality, the very existence of the concentration camp in our technological, color TV, interstate highway, pastel bathroom, jet age, "nice" civilization, is from the cross. Perhaps the only way now we will ever know that we too are judged and reconciled by God, is to recognize Snopes and ourselves in the light of the victory of the resurrected Christ.

13

Two Stories

The two stories that follow revolve about what social scientists, newspapers, political journals, politicians, bureaucrats, welfare workers, and certain kinds of religionists refer to as "the pressing contemporary domestic social issue": the "war" on "poverty." More accurately, these two stories record two responses to the wretched fact that physical poverty does exist in the body politic of affluent and democratic America. It exists in the fact that old men and young women, boys in their teens and girl babies suffer hunger and inadequate diets, disease and physical miseries. The existence of this poverty denies them the possibility to pursue in plenteous and bountiful orders of creation the happiness which they are endowed by their very existence. For the very elementary fact is that they have been denied political and social and legal and economic equity—the "rights" of "life and liberty"—and are thereby deprived, ruthlessly, of the opportunity to earn a decent living in wholesome vocations. In a word, they are denied the very rights this government proclaims itself constituted to guarantee. This poverty is in the body politic not because its victims lack "individual initiative" and "the competitive spirit" but because they are casualties of the very system that makes the "war" on "poverty" a matter of survival to democracy in America.

Physical poverty in the midst of economic affluence breeds spiritual poverty; in some, it takes the form of a callous or calculated indifference to the misery of their brothers; in others, vincible ignorance and social selfishness; in still others, a point of view which accepts their own physical poverty as inevitable and their own situation as beyond hope, so that social scientists now suggest that poverty in America must be understood as a state of mind as well as the absence of a certain amount of income and employment. For centuries moralists have warned that the system of slavery exacted as heavy a toll on the character and personality of the slave-holder as it did upon the slave. Now, perhaps, we need to have them warn us that the toll exacted on the character and personality of the affluent citizen is just as heavy as upon the victims of the affluent society, viz., the poor. In Hosea's words, "they came to Ba'al-pe'or and consecrated themselves to Ba'al, and became detestable like the things they loved."

—The Editors

The Plutocrats and the Po' Folks

WILLIAM PAUL RANDALL

The second section of the Sunday edition of *The Macon Telegraph and News* is "About Women and the Arts" and "The Home and Family Life." The headline on page one reported on Sunday, January 16, that "GREAT SOCIETY POVERTY PROGRAM EVENT ENTERTAINS EXCHANGE CLUB." It did, and it was no accident that it did. The chairman of the party committee was asked by the club to "have something different" for the annual "Ladies' Night" meeting. In the bulletin of the Macon Exchange Club, the plan for "something different" was explained by the chairman: "With the Poverty Program, the Job Corps, the Ladybird Beautification Program, Medicare, unemployment insurance, government by handouts, and money by pipeline from Washington and LBJ, this could well be called 'The Get Age.'. . . As it is almost impossible to beat them, just for tonight we have decided to join them. The Great Society Poverty Program was designed so you may let your hair down, join in the fun and live like po' folks for tonight."

WILLIAM PAUL RANDALL is a contractor in Macon, Georgia, chairman of the Bibb County Co-ordinating Committee, and publisher and editor of *The Macon Weekly*. He is a member of the Church of God and a board member of the Committee of Southern Churchmen.

This kind of program is not something altogether new to Macon. In October 1964 local Republicans staged their "Goldwater Gala," a principal theme of which was a "take-off" on "make-believe poverty." Admission charges were a minimum of $10. The newspaper account of the affair reported that "one song in the 'Appalachia' skit said some people believe the anti-poverty promises because they are 'ignorant, stupid' and another said the people didn't need washing machines because 'they ain't got no clothes to wash nor place to plug 'em in.' " "The ridicule even went so far," the newspaper report continued, as to include a song that said that " 'since they closed Prince Edward's schools, we can't read nor write,' an apparent reference to the county in Virginia where Negroes were without schooling for several years, although there were no blacked faces in the cast." So, the ground for the subsequent effort of the Exchangites to entertain their ladies had already been broken, and success seemed a sure thing.

The spoof party began at the beginning. The newspaper reported that when the guests entered the YWCA, "they faced two doors leading to the banquet room: 'For Plutocrats,' and 'For Po' Folks,' " the reference, apparently, being to the guest "costumed in the spirit of the occasion." Members had been "urged ahead of time to dress for the occasion, either as po' folks or plutocrats."

"Favors for the ladies" were distributed from "sacks of groceries" on which was printed in black and bold letters, "POVERTY PROGRAM."

After members and guests were seated, the banquet was picketed by members of the party committee of the club. Their signs explained what the party was all about: "Spend All Your Pay, There's More on the Way." "Yes, Virginia, There Really is a Santa Claus." "Fly with Lyndon Bird." "LBJ Will Pay Our Way." The menu included peas, crackling bread, and sweet 'tater pudding. But since it was "Ladies' Nite" for the club, the menu also included roast beef, ham, and fried chicken, doubt-less for those with stomachs too delicate to be poor even for a night.

Religion and church were not left out. One sign carried by the pickets read "We uster pray; now we call LBJ." Another said, "Blessed are the Poor, for they have LBJ." The minister of a large congregation, who was "costumed for the Great Society Poverty Program," the newspaper said, sang and chorded his picket: "Never on Sunday"! It was "a feature of the program 'broadcast' from the stage." And, to sum it all up, the Outstanding Exchangite Award was presented to the Master of Ceremonies at the dinner preceding the program, a prominent civic leader in Macon. He was praised for his work "in his church as well as in the club."

In response to all this, one brave parson, in a signed letter to the editor of the Macon *News*, wrote that "one with a shudder suspects that if the Christ of Canaan were to come to Macon, He might find it easier to turn the muddy water of the Ocmulgee River into wine than to turn the water of our callous indifference into the heady wine of God's passionate concern for human need. . . . The billboard injunction, 'Attend the Church of your choice this Sunday,' raises the question: Why? to learn how to laugh?"

Mrs. Combs and the Bulldozers

LOYAL JONES

This is a story about Mrs. Ollie Combs. It is also a story about a community, but mostly it is her story. Mrs. Combs is 61 years old, but in some ways she looks older. She is small and frail and looks weary. But in other ways, she looks younger. She has a quick intelligence, a wry humor, and her smile is still girlish, for she has had her moments of joy. In 1944, she gave birth to triplets, two boys and a girl. Mostly, though, as she puts it, "we lived hard." With her five sons she lives in a small, three-room wooden house under Honey Gap on Clear Creek in Knott County, Kentucky. The house has electricity and television, but is heated by coal in fireplaces. When a stiff wind comes, it sends a draft down through the chimney and blows eye-burning coal dust into the rooms. Yet the rooms are neat, the beds made, the mantles and tables hold family pictures and the Bible, and on one wall hangs a large, woolly, pastel-colored panda bear, wrapped in cellophane to protect it from the coal dust.

Her husband, Balis Combs, a coal miner, died a year ago. A month later, her nineteen-year-old son died. Another son, Jimmy Lee, an Army veteran, has been almost

LOYAL JONES is Director of the Appalachian Center at Berea College, Kentucky. From 1958 to 1970 he was Associate Director, and Director, of the Council of the Southern Mountains.

totally paralyzed since an automobile accident six years ago. Most of the time he is confined to a bed in the front room off the kitchen, but the other boys are able, occasionally, to take him out for a ride. The youngest son, Barney, 13, is in school. Lincoln, 17, and two of the triplets, Jesse and Elmer, 22, are unemployed. Mrs. Combs and her five sons live on Social Security and on the small disability allowance Jimmy Lee receives from the state of Kentucky.

* * *

This particular story about Mrs. Combs really began a long time ago, when a mining company bought the mineral rights to the land on which the Combses lived. The agreement involved a "broad form" deed, which gave the mining company the right to do anything necessary to the surface of the land in order to get at the minerals beneath the surface. Mrs. Combs "owns" the surface of the land, but not the minerals; hence, the mining company can "strip" the surface of the land which she owns in order to get at what they own.

On Monday, November 22, 1965, bulldozers from the Caperton Coal Company pushed through the trees of Honey Gap and onto Mrs. Combs' land. The dozers were following one of the seams of coal which runs around the mountain that rises almost abruptly in the back and side of Mrs. Combs' home. This is "strip mining," and the technique is quite simple. The bulldozers push trees and rocks and earth off the seam of coal, and then power shovels scoop up the coal from whatever depth it might be found. There is no place for the trees and rocks and earth—the "overburden"—to go except to plummet down the mountain, crushing and polluting and destroying whatever might be in the path, until the "overburden" runs its course. For every foot of coal mined by this technique, up to four feet of earth and rocks as well as trees stripped by the dozers pour down the mountain. The point was very simple: had the bulldozers continued to strip, the home of the six members of the Combs family would have been rendered inhabitable, if not swept away, by the "overburden."

So Mrs. Combs stopped the bulldozers. She climbed the steep hill between her home and Honey Gap, and sat down in their path, despite a court injunction against picketing or interfering with mining operations.

And she talked to the drivers: "We live hard. This land and this house is all we've got. Go on and leave us alone."

The president of the mining company, William Caperton, came to the Gap to reason with her. He appealed to Law and Order: "The law's on our side. We have a restraining order to keep you folks off the strip sites."

"It's not worth the paper it's written on," Mrs. Combs responded.

"I've never been stopped yet," Mr. Caperton warned.

"Neither have I," she said, and she continued to talk.

The bulldozers withdrew. The "High" Sheriff, "Bud" Hylton, a deputy, and two state patrolmen came to the scene at Honey Gap, and arrested Mrs. Combs, and her sons Jesse and Lincoln. She instructed the boys to go with the officers peaceably, but she stayed where she was, seated in the middle of the path the dozers had abandoned. Finally, the Sheriff and a state trooper picked her up, and started down the almost sheer path with their burden, still arguing with her. As she recalls it, about halfway down, the puffing "High" Sheriff complained, "Mrs. Combs, if you'll walk, I'll buy you a cup of coffee when we get to town."

"I don't drink coffee," she replied, although later she wryly confessed that this was not so; she did like coffee.

At any event, they had to carry her down the mountain, and they put her in the patrol car and drove her to the county seat of Knott County, Hindman. Her bond was signed, and she was released.

The next day she heard the bulldozers again, at the same spot in Honey Gap. Again she trudged up the mountain to the Gap, and again she sat down in front of the dozers. Again she was arrested, carried off and released on bond. Bill Strode, a photographer from the *Louisville Courier-Journal* who had been taking pictures of the action, was arrested on a "John Doe" warrant for trespassing and put in jail for three and a half hours until his bond was made.

On the day before Thanksgiving, Mrs. Combs halted the bulldozers for a third time. She and her sons were arrested for a third time, and again she was carried off down the mountain. This time, however, she and Jesse and Lincoln were taken before Circuit Judge Don Ward at Hazard, Kentucky. The three were sentenced to twenty hours in jail for violating the court injunction, beginning immediately and running almost to the full Thanksgiving Day.

When the prisoners and the High Sheriff arrived at the jail in Hindman, the Sheriff asked Mrs. Combs to walk into the jail. "My back hurts," he explained.

"You started this business," she answered, "and if you want me in that jail, you're going to have to carry me into it." Later, she recalled that the idea of refusing to walk into the jail had only occurred to her on the trip from Hazard to Hindman.

So the Sheriff had a problem. He called some townspeople to help carry Mrs. Combs into the jailhouse. One of the Combs boys said, within their hearing, "Mama's pretty mad." So the townspeople strolled away from the Sheriff with Mrs. Combs still seated in the car. He tried one of his prisoners, but after hearing what was expected of him, he declined. It seems his back hurt, too. Finally, the Sheriff located a deputy, and the two of them carried her to a cell. The next day after Thanksgiving dinner of chicken and dumplings prepared by the jailor's wife, Mrs.

Buddy Calhoun, she and sons Jesse and Lincoln were released.

"They treated me real good," she explained.

Her neighbors looked after the sons who had to remain at home up Clear Creek.

The influential *Louisville Courier-Journal* gave day by day coverage of Mrs. Combs' encounter with the bulldozers, including a remarkable series of photographs by Bill Strode. Other newspapers and radio and television in the area picked up the story. Governor Edward W. Breathitt issued a statement urging strip miners to stop their insistence upon a strict interpretation of "broad form" deeds. He announced that he was on the side of the small landowners in controversy with the coal companies, and promised to introduce a new strip mine control bill. Judge Ward, who had passed the sentence on Mrs. Combs and her sons, then ordered into immediate effect the more stringent strip mine regulations which had passed the legislature earlier and were due to go into effect on December 18.

William Caperton agreed, for his part, to abide by the new regulations, and stated that he would not mine coal on Mrs. Combs' property. He might, he said, cut a road on the mountain that rises above her home to haul coal mined on adjoining property. Cutting the road, however, would have exactly the same effect as stripping the coal seam. The overburden of trees, rocks, and dirt would ruin her home. Hence, her reaction to this was the same as before: "I'm ready to go back up there again, if they come back."

At any rate, Governor Breathitt was as good as his word. He journeyed to Pennsylvania to study the effect of their strip mine reclamation laws. When the Legislature reconvened, he presented them with a strong strip mine bill. He arranged to have the legislators visit the strip mine fields in Kentucky and to fly to Pennsylvania to see what had been done with their law.

Mrs. Combs went to Frankfort in mid-January to testify before the Legislature on the strip mine bill. In her quiet but emphatic way, she explained to the legislators how, and why, she had stopped the bulldozers, and what she thought about strip mining.

"It's destroying the land. It's poisoning the water. There should be something done to stop them from destroying what people have got, from destroying their homes and their land. I stopped them, if only they stay stopped."

She was applauded by the lawmakers when she finished her statement. They passed a bill which forbids strip mining on slopes steeper than thirty degrees, and requires a greater effort to restore the land which has been stripped.

A few days later, the governor offered another bill seeking to invalidate the despised "broad-form" deeds. His bill argued that when the mineral rights had been sold some fifty to eighty years ago, the sellers could not have foreseen the present-day methods of extracting minerals by means of strip mining. He proposed that only the techniques known at the time the deeds were sold could be employed, without additional consent of current surface owners, and without adequate compensation. The bill was promptly called "The Widow Combs Bill." But the bill was tabled, and was not revived before the session of the legislature adjourned. The most enthusiastic and optimistic supporters for the elimination of the "broad-form" deed see little prospect for passage in the near future. At present, the fate of those threatened by strip mining, such as Mrs. Combs and her five sons, rests with the new law, the diligence of its enforcement, public opinion and interest, particularly in the localities affected by indiscriminate stripping, and the whim or enlightenment of the coal companies. It is clear that the effort to eliminate the ravages and wastes of human and natural resources produced by strip mining is far from over.

Mrs. Combs stopped the bulldozers from pushing through Honey Gap and destroying the home of her family. Because she did this, she helped to get a bill through the legislature of Kentucky which will help others who face the same peril that she faced and met. And it is important to this story to remember that Mrs. Combs was not alone—that support by her neighbors was not exhausted by bringing Thanksgiving dinner to the jail at Hindman. Taken together, the story of Mrs. Combs and her neighbors is one demonstration of what the victims of poverty can do when they act together to meet a common problem. Mrs. Combs' neighbors, the people of Clear Creek and Lotts Creek, supported her defiance of the bulldozers of the Caperton Mining Company. They kept her in sight as she sat in protest in front of the dozers, and confronted the miners, and the law itself. They cheered her on, they looked after her boys while she was in jail, and they saw to it that she had something tangible to be thankful for on Thanksgiving Day besides being a prisoner in the Knotts County jail. These same neighbors, at least some of them, have defied the bull-dozers on their own land, with other techniques, including the use of firearms.

When the "War on Poverty" came to Knott County, the people of Lotts and Clear Creeks came together and formed a neighborhood council. They saw, or thought they saw, rays of hope in the Economic Opportunity Act. The problems of the bulldozers gave impetus to their activities. In the meetings of the neighborhood council, the people talked bitterly of the ruin left by the strip miners as they pushed the top of the mountain off "Number Nine," as the seven- to nine-foot coal seam at the top of the mountain was called. Literally, the top of the mountain—the "overburden"—rolled down the slopes, covering trees and underbrush, and sending dirt and boulders into streams, and fields, and even buildings.

"Why should we be using government to improve

things," someone complained, "when the strip miners will come and destroy all that we have done?"

Everyone in the neighborhood council agreed that strip mining was the most urgent problem they faced. And they agreed that something had to be done. So they created an organization called "The Appalachian Group to Save the Land and People." They retained Harry Caudill, the Whitesburg attorney already famous for his wrangling with the strip miners and for his book, *Night Comes to the Cumberlands*. LeRoy Martin, a schoolteacher, was elected president. Alice Slone, director of Lotts Creek Community School, which most of the children on the Creek attend, insisted that the word "people" be in the name of the group. Miss Slone founded the community school 33 years ago with the help of the small landowners in the area. She had seen bulldozers destroy 40 acres of the school's timber, including two acres of white pine which the schoolchildren had set out as a conservation example for the community. Miss Slone helped in the founding of the group, but she insists that it was mostly the work of the people of Clear and Lotts Creeks. "They were the small farmers and landowners who felt that they had to come together to protect their homes and property from ruin," she said. In many cases the property they sought to defend was, literally, their last chance to avoid becoming wards of the state or their relatives.

They were people like Mrs. Combs—Clarence and Clara Williams and Ruthie Smith—who successfully fought the strip miners. There was Red Singleton who "let lightning strike" the bridge across his creek to keep the bulldozers off his property. Dan Gibson stood with a rifle in front of the property of his stepson who is in Vietnam. He kept off not only the miners but also the sheriff, deputies, and state police who came with a machine gun, carbines and pistols to remove him. "I don't want any trouble," he said. "I'm 81 years old, and I'm ready to die. If I leave, the undertaker will take me. We don't want our homes destroyed and our water polluted. Do any of you want to die? If so, just try to move me." Mr. Gibson won. Incidentally, the miners had no permit to strip his step-son's property, and were on the wrong land.

The Appalachian Group to Save the Land and People piled into cars and went to Frankfort and picketed the Capitol. The governor was impressed, and became a student of the strip mine control and reclamation laws.

Then the bulldozers of the Caperton Coal Company pushed through Honey Gap and onto Mrs. Ollie Combs' property. Indignant, determined, and with nowhere else to go, she stopped the strippers from destroying her home, but she was arrested for the effort. And jailed also was Bill Strode, staff photographer for the *Louisville Courier-Journal*, who refused the order of the Sheriff to stop taking pictures of the incident connected with the arrest of Mrs. Combs. These arrests were costly to the strip miners. National broadcasting networks sent camera crews to the region, as did the British Broadcasting System. *Life* and other magazines and newspapers sent writers and cameramen. Mrs. Combs, and others, who faced bulldozers or guns one day saw themselves as heroes the next day.

The victory of Mrs. Combs and the people of Clear Creek and Lotts Creek is an important one, albeit temporary. Their victory was wrung out of a situation when their backs were to the wall. Abstractions and invocations about freedom or peace, the rights of life and liberty were of no avail. As they saw it, the only choice they had was to put their lives in the gap between the promise and the reality of American democracy. From the point of view of "law and order," the state was simply an instrument to sanction the destruction of their homes. Mrs. Combs had already lost a great deal that had made her life important. The security she had left for herself and for her five sons was the two bedrooms and kitchen under the mountain. She accepted the fact that the weal of her children—of the crippled Jimmy Lee, of Barney and Jesse and Elmer and Lincoln—depended upon what happened when those bulldozers came through Honey Gap. Stripping above her home would surely have ruined what little she did have left—including the possibility of keeping the family together.

It was no easy thing for Mrs. Combs to go down to the meetings of the Appalachian Group to Save the Land and People or to speak before the legislators. It was even more difficult for her to defy physically the bulldozers.

But the way she looks at it is, "You never know what you can stand until it's put on you."

PART 4

14

The End of the World

JAMES Y. HOLLOWAY

> The Pharisees also with the Sadducees came, and tempting
> desired him that he would shew them a sign from heaven. He
> answered and said unto them, when it is evening, ye say, It
> will be fair weather: for the sky is red. And in the morning,
> It will be fair weather today: for the sky is red and lowring.
> O ye hypocrites, ye can discern the face of the sky; but can
> ye not discern the signs of the times? A wicked and adul-
> terous generation seeketh after a sign; and there shall be no
> sign given unto it, but the sign of the prophet Jonah. And he
> left them, and departed.

Consider Apocalypse: that is, heed as the Bible the end
of the world.

We need to take seriously Jesus' warning that there is a
difference between interpreting "the face of the sky" and
discerning "the signs of the times." Most of us have
staked our lives on convictions that read what Jesus
called "the face of the sky." But when we are at the end
of the world, Jesus says, we are evil and adulterous to
interpret "the face of the sky" and claim that we are
discerning "the signs of the times."

To read "the face of the sky" for "the signs of the
times" is to say that if we have made an occasional good

guess about the weather we can prophesy what God is going to do *with us*. To read "the face of the sky" for the "signs of the times" is to live appearances for reality, to live means as end. And this is just what we have been doing in the twentieth century. And this is death. This is the end of the world.

The signs of the times can be discerned only by Jesus' notification that there is *no* sign except the sign of Jonah. That is, the sign of the kingdom of resurrection and reconciliation. The sign that with Christ's own death and resurrection God has already done *for us* what we in our disbelief persist in trying (and failing) to do for ourselves and each other with plans, programs, strategies, relevancies, doings-and-not-doings. He brought us together, with himself, and with all others. We are no longer enslaved to the deadly injunctions "to do" anything about *that.* *That's* done. *That* is not an ideal to work for or a principle to achieve. It is a *fact. The* fact. We are empowered to be what we are, what God has made us: witnesses to what God has done in Christ. We are authorized to be a sign of God's grace that resurrects and reconciles "while still in life" (II Corinthians 5:15). We can be signs of the sign of Jonah. The sign of Jonah means that our world is at an end and there is gospel. There is Good News.

That sign—and only that sign—requires us to interpret the signs of *our* times, and that is to discern the end of the world. *Our world*, not God's Kingdom. Our world: all of our nice artifacts, practices, moralities, cultural gestures, principles, and theories that define our relationships to one another in family, religion, sex, politics, education, war, business, friendships, etc. To interpret the signs of the times is not Ph.D. dissertations, but apocalypse: the end of this world is the end of us. The end of the world is the sign that God in Christ is the end of space, time, history, death, and life.

It is the end of the world when, as Hosea prophesied, our sins do not permit us to return to God: to reach that point in our time when we are unable to do anything but spend our energies in serving ourselves. John the Baptist discerned the same signs when he preached the apocalyptic "fire to come" and the "axe at the root of the tree." The very "fruits that befit repentance" were just the fruits that his people could *not* bear: sharing clothes with the naked and food with the hungry, practicing honesty, and shunning violence in public life. And the Son of Man himself said that when we can only live for ourselves we shall lose our lives.

Consider specifics: the enthusiasm with which we spend millions of lives and trillions of dollars to anticipate and fight the world wars of our century and yet stand powerless, unable to stop the momentum to carnage so that we can lean over and pull from the ditch a few of the victims of three-fourths of the world's population who, due to our passion for war, live in misery and degradation. It is the end of the world because most of us suspect it is un-American, queer, anti-Christ, and bad theology even to consider an end to political killings that leave death and horror in the ditches of the technological era. Consider the end of the world in the police state: the energy and certainty with which we white, liberal Americans encourage the defenders of law and justice as we are piped (and pipe ourselves) into a technological, racist police state so that "we" can be saved from "them." It is the end of the world when people and institutions— especially the institutions of religion, politics, education, and technology—are able only to turn on themselves and on those they were created to serve, and in "the end" only dehumanize and destroy.

A word of vigilance is necessary. We must be careful not to talk cheaply when we talk about the end of the world and overlook the fact that what is at the end is *us,* not the abstractions "culture," "civilization," "life-style," or even "party," "bureaucracy," or "denomina-tion." Characteristics of the end of the world are detach-ment, objectivity, abstraction, impersonality, uncommit-ment. Detachment today is the guile employed by the affluent to leech off the misery of the oppressed and powerless. Objectivity authorizes us to put on the armor of sophistry and to sponsor institutes, courses of study, specialists, books of readings, television documentaries, guided tours, presidential commissions, syllabi, and semi-nars about human misery. These same objectivities never encourage the study of the blasphemies of *our* affluence, opulence, arrogance, cruelty, and heartlessness. Lack of commitment permits us to titillate the conscience of the white, upper-income Americans (which is another way of saying the mass media or higher education) with studies of "crises" out there, but never the crises we *are*.

But to heed the end of the world through the sign of Jonah is not to be concerned with "crises," with the end of culture, civilization, bourgeois or proletarian morality and life-style. Apocalypse is about human beings, about ourselves and what we are doing and have done to others and what is being done to us. The end of the world is not the end of an abstraction, some principle, a cause over there, out yonder, away from *us*, involving only *them*. When it is the end of the world, it is not abstractions and principles that end; it is we—brothers and wives, mothers and fathers and first-borns, those who are near us. It is the end, too, of all the relationships we have with those who are close to us: father and daughter, friend and friend, mother and son, teacher and student, soldier and officer, man and woman, chiefs and clerks, lover and lover. When it is the end of the world, law and order, generation gap, crises on the campus, new morality, sex-ual revolution, death of God, Agnewism, Maoism, Mickey Mouse, Weathermen, Billy Graham in the East Room, hydrogen bombs, Berrigans pursued by scores of FBI agents—all these are "low'rings of the face of the sky." They are signs of "a wicked and adulterous generation" seeking after a sign.

* * *

Religion is both/and; it is blasphemy, when the world is at the end. Politics is either/or; law is bribery; order, tyranny. Music is technique. News, non-news. Education is brainwashing, adjustment to inhumanity. Schools the scene so accurately explained by Rap Brown where you practice what you have learned in the streets. Schools are the marketplace for dope, pills, trafficking in brutality, violence, and frustration; they are eight-to-ten-year prison sentences that disintegrate the cheer and corrupt the soul of the youth of the ghetto and suburb and countryside; they are sixteen-year game preserves for the children (and tenured, political sinecures for the adults) of the affluent societies. Sex is harlotry, business, death, hateful, technical, religious. Caesar is Christ; Christ, Caesar. Art is perversion, commercial.

When it is the end of the world, power is value and its goal, efficiency. The powerful use power to slaughter and control the powerless. Friendship is ideological, connivance. The threats of crises perpetrate the very forces precipitating the crises. World wars slaughter millions to free them; war is our passion, our characteristic, the business of our business and our business is very good. The miracles of modern medicine destroy and maim; to breathe is to risk disaster. Language lies, indoctrinates, perverts. Reason and security require that "the enemy" be killed a hundred times over. Prison is the paradigm of freedom (the Berrigans. Jesus began his ministry only "after John was arrested," and in the end could himself only be arrested). Means are worshiped and ends are in the service of means. Children are the ones who discern "the signs of the times": adults, only "the face of the sky" (consider, as we must, apocalyptically our Lord's resolution in answer to his followers' question about who is "greatest" in the Kingdom: "except ye be converted, and become as little children, ye shall not enter into the Kingdom of heaven").

When the world is at the end, God is dead and America lives! Old Glory shrouds the Cross. Jesus remains in the tomb and it is Up With People! The moon looks down in blood and even the computer, like John the Baptist, knows what we ought "to do": *Repent!* but unlike John cannot tell us *why* we cannot "do" the very thing we must if we are to be saved from the fire that is to come and the axe already laid at the root of the tree.

We dare not take comfort at the end of the world with assurances that "the world has always been like this; this is what it means to be human, perhaps even to 'come of age.' " Instead, we say: "*Who* says the world has 'always been'? And who knows *how* the world has 'always been'? The historians? The philosophers and theologians? No. For they speak only of civilizations, cultures, patterns, life-styles. They cannot speak to *us*, now, at the end of the world."

Amos, Jesus, John, Paul, Augustine, and Reinhold Niebuhr warn that the end of the world could be viewed with equanimity, if not downright enthusiasm, by those God elected, if this meant only the end of a culture, a civilization, a political regime. But the end of the world is God's explicit judgment on those whom he elected. It is his sign that The End, like the end of the world, finds its meaning in the sign of Jonah . . . and in the New Testament—not to leech upon, but to listen unto; to serve, not to use. To discern the signs of the times is to know that we have been called to live under the judgment of the end of the world. There is no longer ethics or morality, culture or civilization, political options or legal safe-guards. There is only the call to live the sign of Jonah that liberates us for everyone—no questions asked!

For such is the Kingdom of God at the end of the world.

Surely I come quickly.
Amen. Even so, come, Lord Jesus.

Katallagete!

15

The Rainbow Sign

PETE YOUNG

> *A new crop comes along every year. . . . It's later than you think. . . . You'd be surprised, without our robes on we look just like people. . . .*
>
> Dragon J. R. (Bob) Jones, 1968

> *We lost the Civil War 'cause our rocks give out.*
>
> A youth from Ormondsville,
> North Carolina, 1965

What follows is a slight revision of the final report I filed as a consultant to the President's Commission on Violence (specifically, the Task Force on Political Assassination). My principal contribution to the work of the Commission was a mass of documentary material, most of it on tape and most of it from old friends in the North Carolina Klan, who showed an amazing willingness to cooperate. The Commission on Violence was stacked with the usual academic types who churned out esoteric

PETE YOUNG covered the resurgence of the North Carolina Klan for a television station in Raleigh. He is completing a book on the white ghetto.

studies on numerous specialized subjects. I sought instead to gather up the raw voices of contemporary anger.

Now it is 1970, and all of the trends so painfully evident in 1968 have ripened by two more years. We are just that much closer to the war of each against all. Currently, the people I have chosen to speak *to*—which is quite different from saying that they have appointed me to speak for them—that is, the low-income whites, are turned on by the great hippie menace. Lynch-a-hippie is now the new panacea for what ails us, and reports of *Easy Rider* encounters are numerous. But as with "nig-ger-knocking," I suspect it won't be too long before even the most ferocious hardhats recognize that lynch-a-hippie is no substitute for structural change.

I suppose the root of our problem is a galloping technology which advances (if that is the term) without conscious direction from the government which would ameliorate the numerous and painful consequences for ordinary citizens.

I do not think there is any possibility of destroying this technology with a new Luddite Rebellion; no more than the egg can be stuffed back into the chicken. There is only a going forward where technology is concerned, hopefully forward to a future where technology is the useful servant of all of the people.

In 1960 Terry Sanford ran for governor of North Carolina on the platform of bringing that fine state into the "American mainstream." Shortly after his election, but several years before I wandered into the first Ku Klux cow pasture, it occurred to me to ask Sanford this question: "Why do we want to get into the 'American mainstream' if it's polluted?" I forget what his answer was, but I think it is still possible for a wide variety of determined groups to carve out little interstices in which experimentation can continue with alternatives to the terrible pollution, both literal and symbolic, of the "American mainstream." I really never knew any "extremists" in the North Carolina Klan; I trained myself to see only a large number of wounded folks struggling to survive in a very extreme time. No doubt the North Carolina Klan continues to go through its various factional gyrations; the hard fact remains that for a "white ghetto" of perhaps two million Tar Heels, Governor Sanford's resurrection of the "New South" dream proved as ephemeral as cotton candy. And, irony of ironies, tragedy of tragedies, the Ku Klux who fled Terry Sanford's "mainstream" proved to be more deeply rooted in the American mainstream than he was!

* * *

I happen to agree with the distinguished black writer, Mr. James Baldwin, on a number of points, principally that unless we soon start telling the truth (as best we can)—about each other, *to* each other and about ourselves—this country of ours is going to dissolve into a quivering spasm of multiple civil wars followed by some form of totalitarianism.

In the midst of a revolutionary *process*, one's own version of the truth depends critically on the vantage point. As it happens, my chosen vantage point is deep within some dusty North Carolina cow pasture—surrounded by the men, women and children of "the white ghetto." Ultimately, I am accountable to *them*. This does *not* require me to endorse certain aspects of their lifestyle, which I regard as pathological. It *does* require that I oppose to the end those who regard the behavior of white ghetto citizens as an inexplicable perversion brought to this innocent country by a demented, racist stork.

This country is not innocent, nor are those who own it and run it. Neither wealth nor power have been distributed equitably. The most solemn promises have not been kept, and the land is now littered with human wreckage. Yes, there is violence and hatred abroad in the land. And there is more to come. Naturally. Why did we expect anything else?

Group behavior, which is "extremist," finds its lowest common denominator in the reality of *powerlessness.* This goes for the white ghetto, the black ghetto and the rebellious young—to name just three of the groups which are now in motion towards a new distribution of the wealth and the power. The young theoreticians of the Students for a Democratic Society, led by Tom Hayden, were quite correct in 1962 when they drafted a manifesto at Port Huron, Michigan, which called for "participatory democracy." Denied realistic access to channels of expression within the formal society, various groups first retreated to form a veritable community-within-the-community, then came charging back in to open up *new* channels with a variety of crude, ugly, vulgar, often illegal techniques.

The angry men, women, and children of the white ghetto—rather thoughtlessly abandoned some years ago by the formal society—turned in upon themselves, examined their own limited resources and then "got their own thing together" with the current edition of an organizational structure that is known commonly (if somewhat misleadingly) as *The Klan.*

In order to protect such lucrative opportunities as come with the tourist trade and industrial development, Southern leaders have tended to minimize the importance of this phenomenon. A nice example of this was provided in North Carolina in 1965, when Governor Dan K. Moore said there were only "618 hard-core Klansmen" in the Tar Heel State. The Governor defined a hard-core Klansman as one who would drive hundreds of miles each week to attend Klan rallies and transact Klan business, all without pay, as a sort of labor of love. Dragon J. R. (Bob) Jones quite correctly replied that if the Governor's own definition were accepted, then there were more "hard-core" Klansmen in the state than hard-core Democrats or Republicans. Silence from the mansion in Raleigh, as Governor Moore sadly reflected on the fact that his king had been trumped by a Klan deuce.

A similar game is played on the national level, probably for reasons of world prestige. The gaping wounds of American black people can no longer be denied; but it is still possible for a little while longer yet to maintain the fiction that this is an isolated case and that the ordinary white American is doing very well indeed in this heavenly paradise of free enterprise and democracy. But truth will out—in fact, it already has—and it is a grim truth full of the most dangerous implications not only for this country but for the entire world.

The night before he was murdered, Dr. King mentioned—just in passing, on his way to the mountaintop—"our sick white brothers."

I want to describe three rather spectacular examples of this sickness.

In late 1963, the civil rights movement focused for a brief period of time on a town in North Carolina. One of the principal targets was a restaurant on the outskirts of town, operated by a man and his wife. Several rather vigorous demonstrations were conducted there. In the course of one of these demonstrations, a young white student demonstrator lay down on the floor. Before the police could arrive to haul him out, the wife of the restaurant owner squatted over the young man, pulled aside her panties and urinated on him.

In the spring of 1965, a young Klansman in the Raleigh area was spending a rare night at home with his wife, their two little children, and a couple of friends. The television program they were watching was suddenly interrupted for a special report from President Johnson, who had earlier that day committed "American boys" in the defense of freedom to the Dominican Republic. The young Klansman dove for his living room closet, came up with a shotgun, and had to be physically restrained by his friends from blasting his own TV set to smithereens.

In the fall of 1966, a small number of black children attempted to integrate the public schools of a certain Mississippi community. These children were assaulted by a mob of white *men,* armed with baseball bats and tire chains. One black child, age 11, had his leg broken. As he crawled away from his bizarre battlefield, he was beaten mercilessly about the head and buttocks.

Now, is there *anybody* who will contend that the incidents I have described were the ordinary criminal actions of ordinary criminals? No, obviously not. These were extraordinary actions committed by citizens who had previously been very ordinary indeed, but who now at this point in time were utterly berserk.

There are those who will say that such remarkable behavior represents the full and final flowering of the "white racist" psychosis. (The young Klansman who wanted to take a shot at the picture of the President on his TV tube was recalling Mr. Johnson's famous "we shall overcome" speech to a joint session of the Congress; this speech outweighed the tattered "fight Communism" banner which the President waved to justify his Dominican intervention.) There can be no doubt that at the time of the actions I have described, the aggressive people involved were, quite literally, foaming at the mouth with expressions of hatred for "niggers." Yet I keep hearing the voice of a Virginia Klan officer saying to me in the same year of 1965:

"We do *not* hate niggers! When are you going to get *that* through your thick stubborn skull?"

This Virginia Klan officer was not trying to con me. What then did he mean?

I think he meant that he had lived his entire life on terms of some intimacy with black people, that he regarded all of them, *as a group,* as inferior to himself. One hates peers. One does not "hate" a faithful family dog, who suddenly stands up on his hind legs and demands equal treatment. One merely kills such a dog, with regret, because it was for years and years a member (subordinate) of the family.

One slumbers for years with the *latent* racism that one's black neighbors are inferior animals; when this incorrect perception of reality is challenged, the racism becomes overt and is often then a license to kill. Hatred doesn't enter into it (according to the Virginia Klan officer). "Niggers" are unworthy of hate, or any other human emotion for that matter.

But at some level of his being, the white ghetto citizen knows he is living a lie. Dimly, he recalls his many human contacts with black people all along the twisted trail of his life. He *is* on fire with hatred, as the result of a difficult life in an impoverished environment; this diffused hatred is suddenly focused on "the nigger," as if the latter were a lightning rod for all the ailments of the world. Yet in the very act of picking up his gun and acting out his hatred, the white ghetto citizen protests that it is not "niggers" he *really* hates. And to a considerable extent, he is right. What we call "racism" is more the expression than the cause of the highly contagious, collective psychosis which afflicts the white ghetto these days in epidemic proportions.

Most white Americans (and many black people) have some difficulty in believing that in this prosperous America *white* citizens exist by the millions in an environment which is so lacking in elemental respects as to be fertile breeding ground for hatred which is finally expressed in a murderous racism.

Permit me, then, to quote at some length from the report of a Presidential Commission, the National Advisory Commission on Rural Poverty, which issued its report in *September 1967.* The quoted excerpts are from the Commission's summary of its report:

"Rural poverty is so widespread, and so acute, as to be

a national disgrace, and its consequences have swept into our cities, violently. . . . Our programs for rural America are woefully out of date. . . . They [the programs] were developed without anticipating the vast changes in technology, and the consequences of this technology to rural people. . . . Most rural programs still do not take the speed and consequences of technological change into account. . . . In contrast to the urban poor, the rural poor, notably the white, are not well organized, and have few spokesmen for bringing the nation's attention to their problems. . . . The nation's major social welfare and labor legislation largely bypassed rural Americans. . . . We have been oblivious of the rural poor. . . . Rural poverty in the United States has no geographic boundaries. It is acute in the South, but it is present and serious in the East, the West and the North. Rural poverty is not limited to Negroes . . . whites outnumber nonwhites among the rural poor by a wide margin. . . . Hunger, even among children, does exist among the rural poor. . . . The rural poor have gone, and now go, to poor schools. . . . Unemployment and underemployment are major problems in rural America. . . . Most of the rural South is one vast poverty area. . . . The community in rural poverty areas has all but disappeared as an effective institution. . . ."

Those who profess surprise that an organization such as "The Klan" should emerge from the environment described above are naive. What do they expect? Roses? The language of the Commission's summary is reminiscent of a runaway grand jury indicting the sheriff for keeping an uninhabitable jail. I can add several observations:

1. The appointment of each new Presidential Commission is greeted by most citizens with a withering blast of cynicism. We have had a plethora of Commissions, federal and state, telling us rather precisely what is wrong and what needs to be done. Yet nothing is done; the recom-

mendations are not followed. The problems continue. It is not so much that the recommendations are *ignored;* they are usually good for a "special" from Walter Cronkite. Rather, the System seems *unable* to do what its own best experts proclaim is essential. It is not entirely facetious to suggest that we might need still another Presidential Commission to examine the question of why previous Commissions have proven so ineffective.

2. We hear a great deal of easy talk these days (often from men whose colonial ancestors whirl in their graves) to the effect that "there is never any excuse or justification for violence, no matter how bad conditions may be." It would be more correct, and not at all hypocritical, to say that people's violence is often misdirected in terms of target and frequently counterproductive in terms of result. The fact is that the grievances so well summarized by the Commission on Rural Poverty far exceed those grievances which caused our forefathers to separate (*violently*) from a distant and rather benign king. The same, of course, can also be said, and must be said, for our black and white brothers trapped in the misery of deteriorating cities. It was the Kerner Commission which dissected *that* environment.

3. I am not in the business of comparing misery, of saying that Group A in the southern countryside is more miserable (or less) than Group B in the northern metropolis. I am simply saying that for *both* Group A and Group B—and perhaps Groups C through G as well—the level of unrelieved misery has long since passed the tolerance threshold, and we are therefore—surprise! surprise! —confronted by an explosive level of alienation that is marked by frequent incidents of violence.

4. For the low-income Southern white—whose grievances are numerous, legitimate, and painfully real—it comes therefore as an unbearable shock to hear repeated expressions of governmental concern for the problems of *black* people. Never mind that these expressions are al-

most invariably hypocritical, designed simply for vote-getting purposes. The point is that the low-income Southern white—that *bigot*, that *redneck*, that *racist*, that *hatemonger*—doesn't even get the hypocritical expressions of concern from the government which is also *his*. It is exactly at this point that the average white ghetto citizen displaces his hatred from government officials (where it belongs) to his black neighbors, who also are victims of the very same shell game. This shell game is *profitable* for some; the driving of a deep wedge between ordinary white and black citizens is precisely what perpetuates the power of a tiny minority, the country club elite. Quite often, the Klansman, as indigenous leader in the white ghetto, has a better understanding of this than do his followers. Example: the young preacher at the Klan rally at Four Oaks, North Carolina, shouted to the multitudes—"When they say H...E...W..., they mean *nigger* Health, they mean *nigger* Education, they mean *nigger* Welfare! You and I are just going to have to suffer it out by ourselves, the best way we can, like we always done." But is this Klan preacher, at rock bottom, furious with "niggers" or "them"? To ask such a question is to answer it. And it is similarly no accident that the *overt* expressions of hostility in the 1968 Wallace campaign were always directed at "pseudo-intellectuals, pointy-headed guideline writers," etc.

5. I recall that time in late 1965, when I took a Yankee journalist into a dingy Klavern Hall near Farmville, North Carolina. A casket was on display, and behind the casket was a crudely lettered sign: "Our government is dead." The Klansmen of the area were *not* referring only to the Government of the United States; their sign reached out to encompass all the subordinate jurisdictions right down to Recorder's Court at Snow Hill. It was *all* "dead," as far as they were concerned. Now please do not tell me that these "redneck extremists" are in a lot of trouble with the government. Masses of people do *not*

(by definition) get "in trouble" with their governments. It works the other way around. *Governments* are the ones in trouble when lines of communication break.

* * *

A curious, largely unnoticed, contradiction gnaws at the heart of the Kerner Commission Report. This Report points—correctly, I think—to "white racism" as the principal underlying cause of the wave of "civil disturbances" in 1967. Having identified the problem as one that was (and is) rooted in the *white* community, the Kerner Commission goes on to recommend various massive programs for the *black* community! On things to do in the white community, the Kerner Commission is essentially silent.

Stripped of its jargon, the usual mixmaster blend of sociology and governmentese—the Kerner Commission seems to be playing this old, old song:

White folks become "racist" when they sniff the air and encounter "niggers" who stink. Clean up the "niggers" with all those nice federal funds, and white folks will no longer be "racist."

Remarkable! In other words, the very Presidential Commission that pointed to "white racism" as the cause of our domestic agony ended up by itself putting forward a white racist position that usually is more pungently expressed by Mississippi sheriffs.

W. H. Ferry has said about the Kerner Commission labors:

> The Commission here betrayed first, its whiteness, and second, its lack of political imagination, by which I mean its inability to visualize a new and mutually beneficial relationship between black and white, which would not be either integration or *apartheid* ("Will Black Colonies Be the Final Solution to the Problem of Integration?" *Katallagete*, Spring 1968).

I would assume that the alternative which Mr. Ferry visualizes is that state of affairs expressed by the short-hand slogan, "black power," that is, a considerable measure of autonomy for black communities. Change the slogan from "black power" to *community* power, and you will catch the key demand emanating from the cow pastures and/or the 1968 Wallace campaign. There is wide agreement, even among the so-called "respectables," that it is past time to decentralize the power that has concentrated in Washington and permit it to flow back to the grass roots. And there is the instinctive folk wisdom of the people (white and black) that the cure for power-lessness—and all the irresponsible behavior which goes with that condition—is . . . *power.*

* * *

I have saved for near the end a more specific discussion of the problem of violence, as it relates to the white ghetto.

An environment which is impoverished on all levels—cultural as well as material—obviously breeds violence on a massive scale, almost as a way of life. There is the violence of car wrecks, the violence of Saturday night drinking sprees and squabbles, the violence of hunting accidents, the violence of spouse against spouse, the violence of suicide via alcohol or the pistol and, indeed (and almost as an afterthought), the violence of race against race. This description of violence in the white ghetto is a mirror image of similar conditions in the black ghetto. And for most of the same reasons.

No act of racial violence occurs in the South for which "The Klan" is not blamed. I do not contend that the Klanspeople I have known are Sunday School types, just simple, misunderstood "agrarian reformers." But I will say that most of the Klan leaders I have known have behaved far more responsibly than this society had any right to expect. Further, there has been entirely too much attention paid "The Klan," and this has blocked the possibility of any constructive action in the white ghetto. To paraphrase George Orwell, "All Klans are created equal; but some Klans are more equal than others." We *all* know that some Klan organizations, such as the one in Mississippi under the leadership of Sam Bowers, have been responsible for numerous acts of premeditated criminal violence. But even with the Mississippi militants, it will be more productive to concentrate on the white ghetto *environment* from which this type of aberrant behavior springs.

As for the more narrow problem of assassination, I cannot imagine the Klan officers I have known engaged in a meeting to plot the killing of a national leader. What I *can* imagine is the ease with which a paramilitary team of tough, professional killers can be recruited out of the white ghetto for almost any target with a high enough price on his head. But here the focus shifts from the team, which is almost incidental, to the rich extremist who finances it. I think we have seen this kind of assassination in recent years. Sadly, I think we will see it again. It's just to easy to arrange, too easy to set up, too tempting to resist.

Beyond the assassinations of such national leaders as the Kennedy brothers, Dr. King, Malcolm X and Medgar Evers, there is the related white ghetto phenomenon of "nigger-knocking." I shall define "nigger-knocking" as the random murder of a black citizen, usually on the road, for the purpose of intimidating the local black community. A publicized example was the killing of Army Colonel Lemuel Penn on a Georgia highway in 1965. Unpublicized examples occur frequently on Southern rural roads; the sheriff finds only a black body, with no clues available to hunt down the slayer. As a general rule, law enforcement agencies are virtually helpless either to prevent or to solve this kind of crime.

As lynching became counterproductive—because of the

pervasive influence of television, and also because of the ease with which law enforcement agencies can infiltrate mobs—the grand old Southern sport of "nigger-knocking" came on to take its place. Its *utterly* random quality makes it more effective than lynching as a control device. And the fact that it is executed by only one man, or at most a carload, minimizes the chances of detection.

"Nigger-knocking" tends to preserve local institutional arrangements, but the dull terror it generates is an important addition to the more basic economic factor (mechanization of Southern agriculture) in stimulating the continuing black migration out of the South and into the dry tinder cities of the North. One of the most popular 45 rpm records distributed by the United Klans of America is entitled, "Move Them Niggers North." At every conceivable level of activity, both legal (if reprehensible) and illegal, this remains as a principal and primitive goal of the white ghetto. Said one white supremacist: "Why waste all this poverty money on some nigger kid trying to make him into a good little boy? A ten-cent bullet will make him a good little boy forever."

My own *very* rough estimate would be that several hundred black people die each year in the South as a result of "nigger-knocking." I note also that the technique is spreading to the North, with "nigger-knocking" incidents reported recently in both Cincinnati and Cleveland.

There is a direct link between the gunning down of an unarmed black peasant on the highway, and the slick professionalism which ended the life of Dr. King. *Professionalism takes practice.* And many men, all too many men, of the white ghetto have unquestionably honed their killing skills to a fine cutting edge.

For the record, it should be noted that I have never known a Klan officer to advocate "nigger-knocking," either publicly or privately. The officers I have known are aware (on an off-the-record basis) that "nigger-knocking" is a frequent occurrence. But they are as helpless as everybody else when it comes to describing the remedy, even when (on occasion) they can make a shrewd guess as to which one of "the boys" was out riding with his carbine the night before.

Curiously, the militant black leaders with whom I have discussed "nigger-knocking" are remarkably unconcerned. One mentions several hundred black bodies a year littering the Southern roads, and the black leaders reply: "Hell, we lose that many each year just in Newark because of narcotics or bad housing." This is a way of saying that the *real* victims of "nigger-knocking" are the "nigger-knockers." How sad, how true.

One final aspect of the "nigger-knocking" problem remains to be considered. A local Klan leader in North Carolina told me in September 1968 that he had expelled thirty-nine "drunks, radicals and troublemakers" so far that year from the one unit under his jurisdiction. He added, "And as soon as we get rid of that bunch of bad apples, we found we were getting a better class of members than ever before."

The difficult question is: Where do the drunks, radicals and troublemakers go when they are expelled from Klan groups and cut loose to act on their own? I suspect that in all too many instances they are out on the highway with real guns loaded with real bullets.

It is not generally appreciated (*and it must be*) that the white ghetto has hundreds and thousands of *seriously* disturbed men, all armed, many of whom are alienated even from local Klan organizations.

Dragon J. R. (Bob) Jones is careful to acknowledge a moral responsibility *only* for the actions of dues-paying members of the United Klans of America, Realm of North Carolina. Since the Dragon is under heavy pressure from the United States Government and its subordinate jurisdictions, he sees no reason or incentive—and why should he?—to reach out and claim a moral responsibility for the actions of his white brothers who do not pay dues to the UKA. The fact that many of these disturbed men are "turned on" by the Dragon's rhetoric at cow pasture rallies is only of fleeting concern to him. The Dragon's immediate problems of survival, in the most literal sense, are such that he must define his responsibilities, both moral and legal, very narrowly.

And so we are full circle, back to this society's awesome failure to deal with what the Kerner Commission called "white racism" on any level other than that of ineffective police harassment or liberal sermons in the pulpit. That failure, unless *quickly* remedied, may take more lives than those of Dr. King and Medgar Evers. Indeed, it is not too much to say that the life of this nation is quite literally on the line in those dusty cow pastures of North Carolina. There is enough ill-suppressed ignorance-rage-paranoia in just one of those pastures to blow the lid all the way off this country. And my own alienation is such that in sick moments from time to time I have wished for precisely that.

* * *

What to do, what to do? Perhaps there will be government officials who will ask about the white ghetto that very same question they have asked so many times about the black ghetto: *What in the world do these people want?*

And the answer, of course, is that "those people" want pretty much what everybody else wants: a little piece of turf to call their own, some sense of control over their own lives, a decent minimum of economic security, an end to government harassment and insults. Ordinary folks (white or black) have absurdly simple demands but, paradoxically, these demands cannot be translated into reality without massive changes in our socio-economic-political system.

Quick fixes? I can think of several.

1. *Stop the scapegoating.* The crisis we are in has *not* been caused by five angry Kluxers in North Carolina, thirteen bisexual Trotskyites in the East Village, or even eighty-one promiscuous teeny-boppers in Berkeley. The crisis is systemic: the System has failed to meet the basic needs of several different groups which now, admittedly, are aggravating the situation by throwing handfuls of sand into the delicate machinery.

2. *Lower by several levels police harassment.* All law enforcement agencies must use paid informers, but I believe this practice has gone out of control in America. We now have a police apparatus which rivals anything the Czar of Russia or, for that matter, Joe Stalin ever had. Half the political activists in America are on some government payroll for the purpose of spying on the other half. And this practice will be about as effective here as it was for the Czar, which is to say that it will not be effective at all.

3. *Flood the white ghetto with resource people.* The existing network of social services in the white ghetto is grossly inferior to that provided in the urban black ghetto. There is a desperate need for health and legal services, for skilled family counselors, for dedicated social workers and youth workers, for tough young chaplains, etc. For example, if the emergency is as serious as the Commission on Rural Poverty found it, then the government might well begin by drafting young doctors for two years service at Rural Health Centers, to be run by the US Public Health Service.

4. *Experiment with carefully supervised "cultural exchange" programs within the United States.* Example: What would one hundred North Carolina Klanspeople make of the Central Ward in Newark, or an Indian reservation? If I know the Klanspeople, they might very well decide that the black folks in Newark and the red folks of the reservation needed some—er, ah—*technical assistance*

in how to use guns and bullets in order to get an intolerable situation straightened out quickly. But that's just one of the chances we'll have to take.

5. *Accept the limitations of the political process.* Campbell and Holloway of the Committee of Southern Churchmen have noted that many Christians have gone beyond the old rule that we should "render unto Caesar the things that are Caesar's." All too many of the brethren have permitted Caesar to define the terms on which they would participate in the secular life. That is a fatal error, because it arouses expectations which cannot be fulfilled. The political process is one tool among many—and perhaps not the most important tool at that—for building *community*.

So those are some of the things I think the Government of the United States and its subordinate jurisdictions could be doing. And what *will* it do? Oh, I think it will probably pass a gun control law. And when that doesn't work, then it will move into increasingly severe acts of repression. And after five or ten years of this sort of nonsense—if any of us is still alive—perhaps there will be *another* Presidential Commission, and I will once again be a consultant. Only the *next* time my message to the authorities will be much shorter and simpler:

You blew it. You blew it because you didn't have the guts to go after basic causes; you only went after symptoms. So you deserve everything that is now coming to you. I cannot help you and (even sadder) I cannot find it in my heart to feel sorry for you. You have richly earned your fate.

Mr. James Baldwin, with whom I began this report, is with me now at the end:

> *God gave Noah*
> *The rainbow sign.*
> *No more water,*
> *The fire next time.*

16

Notes for a Novel About the End of the World

WALKER PERCY

A serious novel about the destruction of the United States and the end of the world should perform the function of prophecy in reverse. The novelist writes about the coming end in order to warn about present ills and so avert the end. Not being called by God to be a prophet he nevertheless pretends to a certain prescience. If he did not think he saw something other people didn't see or at least didn't pay much attention to, he would be wasting his time writing and they reading. This does not mean that he is wiser than they. Rather might it testify to a species of affliction which sets him apart and gives him an odd point of view. The wounded man has a better view of the battle than those still shooting. The novelist is less like a prophet than he is like the canary coal miners used to take down into the shaft to test the air. When the canary gets unhappy, utters plaintive cries, and collapses, it may be time for the miners to surface and think things over.

But perhaps it is necessary first of all to define the sort of novel and the sort of novelist I have in mind. By a novel about "the end of the world," I am not speaking of a Wellsian fantasy or a science fiction film on the late show. Nor would such a novel presume to predict the imminent destruction of the world. It is not even interested in the present, very real capacity for physical destruction: that each of the ninety odd American nuclear submarines carries sixteen Polaris missiles, each of which in turn has the destructive capacity of all the bombs dropped in World War II. Of more concern to the novelist are other signs which, if he reads them correctly, portend a different kind of danger.

It is here that the novelist is apt to diverge from the general population. It seems fair to say that most people are optimistic with qualifications—or rather that their pessimism has specific causes. If the students and Negroes and Communists would behave, things wouldn't be so bad. The apprehension of many novelists, on the other hand, is a more radical business and cannot be laid to particular evils such as racism, Vietnam, inflation. The question which must arise is whether most people are crazy or most serious writers are crazy. Or to phrase the alternatives more precisely: is the secular city in great trouble or is the novelist a decadent bourgeois left over from a past age who likes to titivate himself and his readers with periodic doom-crying?

The signs are ambiguous. The novelist and the general reader agree about the nuclear threat. But when the novelist begins behaving like a man teetering on the brink of the abyss here and now, or worse, like a man who is already over the brink and into the abyss, the reader often gets upset and even angry. One day an angry lady stopped me on the street and said she did not like a book I wrote but that if I lived up to the best in me I might write a good Christian novel like *The Cardinal* by Henry Morton Robinson or perhaps even *The Foundling* by Cardinal Spellman.

What about the novelist himself? Let me define the sort of novelist I have in mind. I locate him not on a scale of merit—he is not necessarily a good novelist—but in terms of goals. He is, the novelist we speak of, a writer who has an explicit and ultimate concern with the nature of man and the nature of reality where man finds himself. Instead of constructing a plot and creating a cast of characters from a world familiar to everybody, he is more apt to set forth with a stranger in a strange land where the signposts are enigmatic but which he sets out to explore nevertheless. One might apply to the novelist such adjectives as "philosophical," "metaphysical," "prophetic," "eschatological," and even "religious." I use the word "religious" in its root sense as signifying a radical *bond*, as the writer sees it, which connects man with reality—or the failure of such a bond—and so confers meaning to his life—or the absence of meaning. Such a class might include writers as diverse as Dostoevsky, Tolstoy, Camus, Sartre, Faulkner, Flannery O'Connor. Sartre, one might object, is an atheist. He is, but his atheism is "religious" in the sense intended here: that the novelist betrays a passionate conviction about man's nature, the world and man's obligation in the world. By the same token I would exclude much of the English novel—without prejudice: I am quite willing to believe that Jane Austen and Samuel Richardson are better novelists than Sartre and O'Connor. The nineteenth-century Russian novelists were haunted by God; many of the French existentialists are haunted by his absence. The English novelist is not much interested one way or another. The English novel traditionally takes place in a society as everyone sees it and takes it for granted. If there are vicars and churches prominent in the society, there will be vicars and churches in the novel. If not, not. So much for vicars and churches.

What about American novelists? One would exclude, again without prejudice, social critics and cultural satirists like Steinbeck and Lewis. The Okies were too hungry to have "identity crises." Dodsworth was too interested in

Italy and *dolce far niente* to worry about God or the Death of God. The contemporary novel deals with the sequelae. What happens to Dodsworth after he lives happily ever after in Capri? What happens to the thousand Midwesterners who settle on the Riviera? What happens to the Okie who succeeds in Pomona and now spends his time watching Art Linkletter? Is all well with them or are they in deeper trouble than they were on Main Street and in the dust bowl? If so, what is the nature of the trouble?

We have a clue to the preoccupation of the American novelist in the recurring complaint of British critics. A review of a recent novel spoke of the Americans' perennial disposition toward "philosophical megalomania." Certainly one can agree that if British virtues lie in tidiness of style, clarity and concision, a respect for form, and a native embarrassment before "larger questions," American failings include pretension, grandiosity, formlessness, Dionysian excess, and a kind of metaphysical omnivorousness. American novels tend to be about everything. Moreover, at the end, everything is disposed of, God, man, and the world. The most frequently used blurb on the dust jackets of the last ten thousand American novels is the sentence: This novel investigates the problem of evil and the essential loneliness of man. A large order, that, but the American novelist usually feels up to it.

This congenital hypertrophy of the novelist's appetites no doubt makes for a great number of very bad novels, especially in times when, unlike nineteenth-century Russia, the talent is not commensurate with the ambition.

* * *

Since true prophets, that is, men called by God to communicate something urgent to other men, are currently in short supply, the novelist may perform a quasi-prophetic function. Like the prophet, his news is general-

ly bad. Unlike the prophet, whose mouth has been puri-
fied by a burning coal, the novelist's art is often bad,
too. It is fitting that he should shock and therefore warn
his readers by speaking of last things, if not the Last Day
of the Gospels, then of a possible coming destruction, of
a laying waste of cities, of vineyards reverting to the
wilderness. Like the prophet he may find himself in
radical disagreement with his fellow countrymen. Unlike
the prophet, he does not generally get killed. More often
he is ignored. Or if he writes a sufficiently dirty book, he
might become a best seller or even be bought by the
movies.

What concerns us here is his divergence from the usual
views of the denizens of the secular city in general and in
particular from the new theologians of the secular city.

While it is important to take note of this divergence,
extreme care must be taken not to distort it and especially not to fall prey to the seduction of crepe-hanging
for its own sake. Nothing comes easier than the sepul-
chral manifestos of the old-style café existentialist and
the new-style drop-out who professes to despise the
squares and the technology of the Western city while
living on remittance checks from the same source and
who would be the first to go for his shot of penicillin if
he got meningitis.

Yet even after proper precautions are exercised, it is
impossible to overlook a remarkable discrepancy. It
would appear that most serious novelists, to say nothing
of poets and artists, find themselves out of step with their
counterparts in other walks of life in the modern city,
doctor, lawyer, businessman, technician, laborer, and
now the new theologian.

It's an old story with novelists. People are always
asking, Why don't you write about pleasant things and
normal people? Why all the neurosis and violence? There
are many nice things in the world. The reader is offended.
But if one replies, Yes, it's true, in fact there seem to be

more nice people around now than ever before, but somehow as the world grows nicer it also grows more violent. The triumphant secular society of the Western World, the nicest of all worlds, killed more people in the first half of this century than have been killed in all history. Travelers to Germany before the last war reported that the Germans were the nicest people in Europe. Now the reader is even more offended.

If one were to take a Gallup poll of representative denizens of the megalopolis on this subject, responses to a question about the future might run something like this:

Liberal politician: if we use our wealth and energies constructively to provide greater opportunities for all men, there is unlimited hope for man's well-being.

Conservative politician: if we defeat Communism and revive old-time religion and Americanism, we have nothing to worry about.

Businessman: business is generally good; the war is not hurting much but the Negroes and the unions and the government could ruin everything.

Laborer: all this country needs is an eight-hour week and a guaranteed minimum income.

City planner: if we could solve international problems and spend our yearly budget on education and housing, we could have a paradise on earth.

Etc., etc. Each is probably right. That is to say, there is a context within which it is possible to agree with each response.

But suppose one were to ask the same question of a novelist who, say, was born and raised in a community which has gone far to satisfy the lists of city needs, where indeed housing, education, recreational and cultural facilities are first class; say some such place as Shaker Heights, Pasadena, or Bronxville. How does he answer the poll? In the first place, if he was born in one of these places, he has probably left since. It might be noted in passing that such communities (plus Harvard, Princeton, Yale, Bennington, Sarah Lawrence, and Vassar) have produced remarkably few good novelists lately, which latter are more likely to come from towns in south Georgia or the Jewish sections of New York and Chicago.

But how, in any case, is the refugee novelist from Shaker Heights likely to respond to the poll? I venture to say his response might be something like: *Something is wrong here; I don't feel good.*

Now of course, if all generalizations are dangerous, perhaps the most dangerous of all is a generalization about novelists, who are a perverse lot and don't even get along with each other, and who, moreover, speak an even more confused Babel nowadays than usual. But if there is a single strain that runs through the lot, whether Christian or atheist, black or white, Greek or Jew, it is a profound disquiet.

Is it too much to say that the novelist, unlike the new theologian, is one of the few remaining witnesses to the doctrine of original sin, the imminence of catastrophe in paradise?

If, anyhow, we accept this divergence as a fact, that the serious American artist is in dissent from the current American proposition, we are faced with some simple alternatives by way of explanation.

Either we must decide that the artist is mistaken and in what sense he is mistaken: whether he is a self-indulged maniac or a harmless eccentric or the culture's court jester whom everyone expects to cut the fool and make scandalous sallies for which he is well paid.

Or the novelist in his confused Orphic way is trying to tell us something we would do well to listen to.

Again it is necessary to specify the dissent, the issue and the parties to it. One likes to pick the right enemies and unload the wrong allies.

The issue, one might say at the outset, is not at all the traditional confrontation between the "alienated" artist and the dominant business-technological community. For one thing, the novelist, even the serious novelist who doesn't write dirty books, never had it so good. It is businessmen, or rather their wives, who are his best customers. Great business foundations compete to give him money. His own government awards him cash prizes. For another thing, the old self-image of the artist as an alien in a hostile society seems increasingly to have become the chic property of those writers who have no other visible claim to distinction. Nothing is easier than to set up as a two-bit beat Cassandra crying havoc in bad verse.

It is the grossness of conventional distinctions which makes the case difficult. The other day I received a questionnaire from a sociologist, who had evidently compiled a list of novelists. The first question was something like: "Do you, as a novelist, feel alienated from the society around you?" I refused to answer the question on the grounds that any answer would be certain to be misunderstood. To have replied "yes" would embrace any one of several ambiguities. One "yes" might mean: "Yes, I find the entire Western urban-technological complex repugnant, and so I have dropped out, turned on, and tuned in." Another "yes" might mean: "Yes, since I am a Christian and therefore must to some degree feel myself an alien and wayfarer in any society, so do I feel myself in this society, even though I believe that Western democratic society is man's best hope on this earth." Another "Yes" might mean: "Yes, being a John Bircher, I am convinced the country has gone mad."

The novelist's categories are not the same as the sociologist's. So his response to the questionnaire is apt to be perverse: instead of responding to the questions, he wonders about the questioner. Does the questionnaire imply that the sociologist is not himself alienated? Having achieved the transcending objective stance of science, has he also transcended the mortal condition? Or is it even possible that if the sociologist should reply to his own questionnaire: "No, I do not feel alienated"—that such an answer, though given in good faith, could nevertheless conceal the severest sort of alienation? One thinks of the alienation Søren Kierkegaard had in mind when he described the little Herr Professor who has fitted the entire world into a scientific system but does not realize that he himself is left out in the cold and cannot be accounted for as an individual.

If the scientist's vocation is to clarify and simplify, it would seem that the novelist's aim is to muddy and complicate. For he knows that even the most carefully contrived questionnaire cannot discover how it really stands with the sociologist or himself. What will be left out of even the most rigorous scientific formulation is nothing else than the individual himself. And since the novelist deals first and last with individuals and the scientist treats individuals only to discover their general properties, it is the novelist's responsibility to be chary of categories and rather to focus upon the mystery, the paradox, the *openness* of an individual human existence. If he is any good, he knows better than to speak of the "businessman," as if there were such a genus. It was useful for Sinclair Lewis to create George Babbitt but it has served no good purpose for bad novelists to have created all businessmen in the image of George Babbitt.

Here is the sort of businessman the "religious" novelist is interested in, that is, the novelist who is concerned with the radical questions of man's identity, his relation to God or to God's absence. He sketches out a character, a businessman-commuter who, let us say, is in some sense or other *lost* to himself. That is to say, he feels that something has gone badly wrong in the everyday round of business activity, in his office routine, in the routine life at home, in his Sunday morning churchgoing, in his coaching of the little league. Even though by all objective criteria all is well with him, he knows that all is not well with him. What happens next? Of course he can opt out. But thanks to Sinclair Lewis, we now know better than Sinclair Lewis. One is not content to have him opt out and take up the thong-sandaled life in Capri. Perhaps we do have better sense in some matters. Or perhaps it is only that Capri is too available. As a matter of fact it would be easier nowadays to write a satirical novel about some poor overaged hippie who did drop out and try to turn on. But the present-day novelist is more interested in catastrophe than he is in life among the flower people. Uncertain himself about what has gone wrong, he feels in his bones that the happy exurb stands both in danger of catastrophe and somehow in need of it. Like Thomas More and St. Francis he is most cheerful with Brother Death in the neighborhood. Then what happens to his businessman? One day he is on his way home on the five-fifteen. He has a severe heart attack and is taken off the train at a commuter's station he has seen a thousand times but never visited. When he regains consciousness, he finds himself in a strange hospital surrounded by strangers. As he tries to recall what has happened, he catches sight of his own hand on the counterpane. It is as if he had never seen it before: he is astounded by its complexity, its functional beauty. He turns it this way and that. What has happened? Certainly a kind of natural revelation, which reminds one of the experiences induced by the psychedelic drugs. (It is interesting to note that this kind of revelation, which can only be called a revelation of being, is viewed by the "religious" novelist as exhilarating or disgusting depending on his "religion." Recall Sartre's Roquentin catching sight of his own hand, which reminds him of a great fat slug with red hairs.) At any rate I cite this example to show the kind of character, the kind of predicament, the kind of event with which the novelist is nowadays more likely to concern himself than was Hemingway or Lewis. Is it not reasonable to say that in some sense or other, the stricken

commuter has "come to himself"? In what sense he has
come to himself, how it transforms his relationship with
his family, his business, his church, is of course the
burden of the novel.

* * *

In view of the triumphant and generally admirable
democratic-technological transformation of society, what
is the ground of the novelist's radical disquiet? Can the
charge be brought against him, as Harvey Cox has accused
the existentialists, of being an anachronism, one of the
remnant of nineteenth-century "cultivated personalities"
who, finding no sympathetic hearing from either technician or consumer, finds it convenient to believe that the
world is going to the dogs?

Might not the novelist follow the new theologian in his
embrace of the exurb and the computer? Evidently the
former does not think so. Offhand, I cannot think of a
single first-class novelist who has any use for the most
"successful" American society, namely life in the prosperous upper-middle-class exurb, in the same sense that
Jane Austen celebrated a comparable society. Rather is
the novelist more apt to be a refugee from this very
society.

The curious fact is that it is the new novelist who
judges the world and not the new theologian. It is the
novelist who, despite his well-advertised penchant for
violence, his fetish of freedom, his sexual adventurism,
pronounces anathemas upon the most permissive of societies, which in fact permits him everything.

How does the novelist judge the new theologian? One
might expect that since one of the major burdens of the
American novel since Mark Twain has been a rebellion
against Christendom, the emancipated novelist might
make common cause with the emancipated theologian.
The truth is, or so it appears to me, that neither novelists

nor anybody else is much interested in *any* theologians, and least of all in God-is-Dead theologians. The strenuous efforts of the latter to baptize the computer remind one of the liberal clergyman of the last century, who used to wait, hat in hand so to speak, outside the scientific laboratories to assure the scientist there was no conflict between science and religion. The latter could not have cared less.

Yet the contemporary novelist is as preoccupied with catastrophe as the orthodox theologian with sin and death.

Why?

Perhaps the novelist, not being a critic, can only reply in the context of his own world-view. All issues are ultimately religious, said Toynbee. And so the "religion" of the novelist becomes relevant if he is writing a novel of ultimate concerns. It would not have mattered a great deal if Margaret Mitchell were a Methodist or an atheist. But it does matter what Sartre's allegiance is, or Camus' or Flannery O'Connor's. For what his allegiance is, is what he is writing about.

As it happens, I speak in a Christian context. That is to say, I do not conceive it my vocation to preach the Christian faith in a novel, but as it happens my world-view is informed by a certain belief about man's nature and destiny which cannot fail to be central to any novel I write.

Being a Christian novelist nowadays has certain advantages and disadvantages. Since novels deal with people and people live in time and get in predicaments, it is probably an advantage to subscribe to a world-view which is incarnational, historical and predicamental, rather than, say, Buddhism, which tends to devalue individual persons, things, and happenings. What with the present dislocation of man, it is probably an advantage to see man as by his very nature an exile and wanderer rather than as a behaviorist sees him: as an organism in an environment. Despite

Camus' explicit disavowal of Christianity, his Stranger has blood ties with the wayfarer of St. Thomas Aquinas and Gabriel Marcel. And if it is true that we are living in eschatological times, times of enormous danger and commensurate hope, of possible end and possible renewal, the prophetic-eschatological character of Christianity is no doubt peculiarly apposite.

It is also true, as we shall presently see, that the Christian novelist suffers special disabilities.

But to return to the question: what does he see in the world which at once arouses in him the deepest forebodings and at the same time kindles excitement and hope?

What he sees first in the Western world is the massive failure of Christendom itself. But it is a peculiar failure and he is apt to see it quite differently from the scientific humanist, for example, who may quite frankly regard orthodox Christianity as an absurd anachronism. The novelist, to tell the truth, is much more interested in the person of the scientific humanist than in Science and Religion. Nor does he set much store by the usual complaint of Christians that the enemies are materialism and atheism and Communism. It is at least an open question whether the world which would follow a total victory of the most vociferous of the anti-Communists would be an improvement over the present world with all its troubles.

No, what the novelist sees, or rather senses, is a certain quality of the post-modern consciousness as he finds it and as he incarnates it in his own characters. What he finds—in himself and in other people—is a new breed of person in whom the potential for catastrophe—and hope—has suddenly escalated. Everyone knows about the awesome new weapons. But what is less apparent is a comparable realignment of energies within the human psyche. The psychical forces presently released in the post-modern consciousness open unlimited possibilities for both destruction and liberation, for an absolute loneliness or a rediscovery of community and reconciliation.

The subject of the post-modern novel is a man who has very nearly come to the end of the line. How very odd it is, when one comes to think of it, that the very moment he arrives at the threshold of his new city with all its hard-won relief from the sufferings of the past, happens to be the same moment that he runs out of meaning! It is as if he surrenders his ticket, arrives at his destination and gets off his train—and then must also surrender his passport and become a homeless person! The American novel in past years has treated such themes as persons whose lives are blighted by social evils or of reformers who attack these evils, or perhaps of the dislocations of expatriate Americans, or of Southerners living in a region haunted by memories. But the hero of the post-modern novel is a man who has forgotten his bad memories and conquered his present ills and who finds himself in the victorious secular city. His only problem now is to keep from blowing his brains out.

Death-of-God theologians are no doubt speaking the truth when they call attention to the increasing irrelevance of traditional religion. Orthodox theologians claim with equal justification, though with considerably more dreariness, that there is no conflict between Christian doctrine and the scientific method. But to the novelist it looks as if such polemics may be overlooking the *tertium quid* within which all such confrontations take place, the individual consciousness of post-modern man.

The wrong questions are being asked. The proper question is not whether God has died or been superseded by the urban-political complex. The question is not whether the Good News is no longer relevant, but whether it is possible that man is presently undergoing a tempestuous restructuring of his consciousness which does not presently allow him to take account of the Good News. For what has happened is not merely the technological transformation of the world but something psychologically even more portentous. It is the absorption by the layman not of the scientific method but rather the magical aura of science, whose credentials he accepts for all sectors of reality. Thus in the lay culture of a scientific society nothing is easier than to fall prey to a kind of seduction which sunders one's very self from itself into an all-transcending "objective" consciousness and a consumer-self with a list of "needs" to be satisfied. It is this monstrous bifurcation of man into angelic and bestial components against which old theologies must be weighed before new theologies are erected. Such a man could not take account of God, the devil, and the angels if they were standing before him, because he has already peopled the universe with his own hierarchies. When the novelist writes of a man "coming to himself" through some such catalyst as catastrophe or ordeal he may be offering obscure testimony to a gross disorder of consciousness and to the need of recovering oneself as neither angel nor organism but as a wayfaring creature somewhere between.

And so the ultimate question is, What is the *term* or historical outcome of this ongoing schism of the consciousness? Which will be more relevant to the "lost" man of tomorrow who knows he is lost: the new theology of politics or the renewed old theology of Good News? What is most noticeable about the new theology, despite the somber strains of the funeral march, is the triviality of the postmortem proposals. After the polemics, when the old structures are flattened and the debris cleared away, what is served up is small potatoes indeed. What does the Christian do with his God dead and His name erased? It is proposed that he give more time to the political party of his choice or perhaps to make a greater effort to be civil to sales ladies and shoe clerks. To the "religious" novelist, whether it be Sartre or O'Connor, the positive proposals of the new theology must sound like a set of resolutions passed at the PTA.

The man who writes a serious novel about the end of the world—the passing of one age and the beginning of another—must reckon not merely, like H. G. Wells, with changes in the environment but also with changes in man's consciousness which may be quite as radical. Will this consciousness be more or less religious? The notion of man graduating from the religious stage to the political is after all an unexamined assumption. It might in fact turn out that the modern era, which is perhaps two hundred years old and has already ended, will be known as the Secular Era, which came to an end with the catastrophes of the twentieth century.

The contrast between the world-views of denizens of the old modern world and the post-modern world might be sketched novelistically.

Imagine two scientists of the old modern world, perhaps a pair of physicists at Los Alamos in the 1940s. They leave the laboratory one Sunday morning after working all night and walk past a church on their way home. The door is open and as they pass, they hear a few words of the gospel preached. "Come, follow me" or something of the sort. How do they respond to the summons? What do they say to each other? What can they do or say? Given the exhilarating climate of the transcending objectivity and comradeship which must have existed at the high tide of physics in the early twentieth century, it is hard to imagine a proposition which would have sounded more irrelevant than this standard sermon preached, one allows, with all the characteristic dreariness and low spirits of Christendom at the same time in history. If indeed the scientists said anything, what they said would not even amount to a rejection of the summons—*Come!*—a summons which is only relevant to a man in a certain predicament. Can one imagine these scientists conceiving themselves in a predicament other than a *Schadenfreude* about creating the ultimate weapon? Rather would the words heard at the open door be received as a sample of a certain artifact of culture. Scientist A might say to Scientist B: "Did you know there is a local cult of Penitentes not five miles from here who carry whips and chains in a pre-Lenten procession?" Nor can one blame them for attending such a spectacle in the same spirit with which they attend the corn dance at Tesuque. (The fact is that some of the Los Alamos physicists became quite good amateur ethnologists.)

Imagine now a third scientist, perhaps a technician, fifty years later. Let us suppose that the world has not even blown up—it is after all too easy to set the stage so that the gospel is preached to a few ragamuffins in the ruins. Rather has it happened that the high culture of twentieth-century physics long since subsided to a routine mop-up of particle physics—something like a present-day botanist who goes to Antarctica in the hopes of discovering an overlooked lichen. The technician, employed in the Santa Fe-Taos Senior Citizens Compound is doing routine radiation counts on synthetic cow's milk. But let us suppose that the schism and isolation of the individual consciousness has also gone on apace so that mankind is presently divided into two classes: the consumer long since anesthetized and lost to himself in the rounds of consumership, and the "stranded" objectivized consciousness, a ghost of a man who wanders the earth like Ishmael. Unlike the consumer he knows his predicament. He is the despairing man Kierkegaard spoke of, for whom there is hope because he is aware of his despair. He is a caricature of the contemporary Cartesian man who has objectified the world and his body and sets himself over against both like the angel at the gates of Paradise. All creaturely relations crumble at his touch. He has but to utter a word: "achieving intersubjectivity," "interpersonal relations," "meaningful behavior"—and that which the word signifies vanishes.

Such a man leaves his laboratory on a workaday

Wednesday feeling more disembodied than usual and passes the same church which is now in ruins, ruined both by the dreariness of the old Christendom and the nutty reforms of the new theologians. From the ruins a stranger emerges and accosts him. The stranger is himself a weary flawed man, a wayfarer. He is a priest, say, someone like the whisky priest in Graham Greene's *The Power and the Glory* who has been sent as yet another replacement into hostile territory. The stranger speaks to the technician. "You look unwell, friend." "Yes," replies the technician, frowning. "But I will be all right as soon as I get home and take my drug, which is the best of the conscious-ness-expanding community-simulating self-integrating drugs." "Come," says the priest, "and I'll give you a drug which will integrate your self once and for all." "What kind of a drug is that?" "Take this drug and you will need no more drugs." Etc.

How the technician responds is beside the point. The point concerns modes of communication. It is possible that a different kind of communication-event occurred in the door of the church than had occurred fifty years earlier.

* * *

The American Christian novelist faces a peculiar dilem-ma today. (I speak, of course, of a dilemma of the times and not of his own personal malaise, neuroses, failures to which he is at least as subject as his good heathen col-leagues, sometimes I think more so.) His dilemma is that though he professes a belief which he holds saves himself and the world and nourishes his art besides, it is also true that Christendom seems in some sense to have failed. Its vocabulary is worn out. This twin failure raises problems for a man who is a Christian and whose trade is with words. The old words of grace are worn smooth as poker chips and a certain devaluation has occurred, like a poker chip after it is cashed in. Even if one talks only of Christendom, leaving the heathens out of it, of Christendom where everybody is a believer, it almost seems that when everybody believes in God, it is as if everybody started the game with one poker chip which is the same as starting with none.

The Christian novelist nowadays is like a man who has found a treasure hidden in the attic of an old house, but he is writing for people who have moved out to the suburbs and who are bloody sick of the old house and everything in it.

The Christian novelist is like a starving Confederate soldier who finds a $100 bill on the streets of Atlanta, only to discover that everyone is a millionaire and the grocers won't take the money.

The Christian novelist is like a man who goes to a wild lonely place to discover the truth within himself and there after much ordeal and suffering meets an apostle who has the authority to tell him a great piece of news and so tells him the news with authority. He, the novelist, believes the news and runs back to the city to tell his countrymen, only to discover that the news has already been broadcast, that this news is in fact the weariest canned spot-announcement on radio-TV, more commonplace than the Esso commercial, that in fact he might just as well be shouting *Esso! Esso!* for all that anyone pays any attention to him.

The Christian novelist is like a man who finds a treasure buried in a field and sells all he has to buy the field, only to discover that everyone else has the same treasure in his field and that in any case real estate values have gone so high that all field owners have forgotten the treasure and plan to subdivide.

There is, besides the devaluation of its vocabulary, the egregious moral failure of Christendom. It is significant that the failure of Christendom in the United States has not occurred in the sector of theology or metaphysics, with which, also, the existentialists and new theologians are concerned and toward which Americans have always been indifferent, but rather in the sector of everyday morality, which has acutely concerned Americans since the Puritans. Americans take pride in doing right. It is not chauvinistic to suppose that perhaps they have done righter than any other great power in history. But in the one place, the place which hurts the most and where charity was most needed, they have not done right. White Americans have sinned against the Negro from the beginning, continue to do so, initially with cruelty and presently with an indifference which may be even more destructive. And it is the churches which, far from fighting the good fight against man's native inhumanity to man, have sanctified and perpetuated this indifference.

To the eschatological novelist it even begins to look as if this single failing may be the tragic flaw in the noblest of political organisms. At least he conceives it as his duty to tell his countrymen how they can die of it so that they will not.

What is the task of the Christian novelist who mirrors in himself the society he sees around him—who otherwise would not be a novelist—whose only difference from his countrymen is that he has the vocation to be a novelist? How does he set about writing, having cast his lot with a discredited Christendom and having inherited a defunct vocabulary?

He does the only thing he can do. Like Joyce's Stephen Daedalus he calls on every ounce of cunning, craft, and guile he can muster from the darker regions of his soul. The fictional use of violence, shock, comedy, insult, the bizarre are the everyday tools of his trade. How could it be otherwise? How can one possibly write of baptism as an event of immense significance, when baptism is already accepted but accepted by and large as a minor tribal rite somewhat secondary in importance to taking the kids to see Santa at the department store? Flannery O'Connor conveyed baptism through its exaggeration, in one novel, as a violent death by drowning. In answer to a question about why she created such bizarre characters, she replied that for the near-blind you have to draw very large, simple caricatures.

So too may it be useful to write a novel about the end of the world. Perhaps it is only through the conjuring up of catastrophe, the destruction of all Esso signs, and the sprouting of vines in the church pews, that the novelist can make vicarious use of catastrophe in order that he and his reader may come to themselves.

Whether or not the catastrophe actually befalls us, or is deserved; whether reconciliation and renewal may yet take place, is not for the novelist to say.

17

Our Grade Is "F"

WILL D. CAMPBELL
JAMES Y. HOLLOWAY

From the Niña, the Pinta, and the Santa Maria to the
Mekong Delta, failure is a word never to be tolerated in
American life. Throughout our history, we have always
done whatever was necessary for success, even if we had
to change what the word meant (as yesterday in the wars
against the Indians and today in Vietnam). Yet if one
takes even a casual look at the American scene today,
there is no cause to celebrate our successes. Instead, we
are failing, and there is despair in the land. We are failing
as a people, as a political entity, as a Christian community, and as individual Christians.

* * *

Take the racial question. Writers, reporters, social
scientists, experts on human relations, preachers, rabbis,
and priests who moved into the big and hopeful arena of
integrating American culture ten or twenty years ago are
now slowly and sadly turning to more promising fields of
interest and service—observing or talking about the Sunday afternoon dragstrip, farming, the local pool hall,
crafts, breeding dogs, etc.

Ten years ago it was different. While Southern legislators and reactionary newspaper editors were screaming
"Never!" we liberals were exuding optimism with our
foundation grant and a well-written and organized table
of procedure. The enemy stood as a clear target. The
issues were clearcut. To be sure, there were not a lot of
us, but the task was an obvious one. Get the nine black
children into school. Get Governor Faubus to withdraw
his troops. Get the federal troops here. Get the public
schools open. All those things were accomplished, and
some of us were a part of it. Ten years later things are not
really better in America as far as the problem of race is
concerned. They are worse. And in the name of progress—public housing, urban renewal, and model cities—a
program of resegregation has begun. The target does not
stand so clear today.

Ten years ago a handful of us in the occupied city of
Little Rock, Arkansas, walked to school the first day
with the nine black children. We felt fresh and clean
inside. But today we would hesitate to take that same
walk, not for fear of the National Guard, but for fear of
meeting the jeers of "Honky, go home!"

No longer can we identify the enemy so easily. No
longer can we isolate the issues. We are denied issues. No
longer do we battle against flesh and blood, but against
principalities and powers, spiritual wickedness in high
places. There is despair in the land. There is failure in the
land.

What happened? Perhaps we started too late. Perhaps we
chose the wrong enemy in the first place. Or perhaps, like
Israel, our sins do not permit us to turn to God (Hosea
5:4); perhaps we could not turn from our wicked ways if
we wanted to. There comes a time when even repentance
is impossible and only judgment remains. Perhaps those
we sought to help had already seen too much of us.
Perhaps they alone knew who we really were. They had
seen what Vincent Harding reminds us of: the burning of

the Indians by our Puritan fathers while they gave thanks to God. They had seen the concentration camps we created for those first families. They had seen our rape of Mexico, the crushing of the Cuban rebellion in 1898, and the destruction of the Philippine revolution in the years that followed. They had watched our constant domination of the Latin nations. They heard the accusation by one of their leaders that World War I was primarily the jealous and avaricious struggle for the larger share in exploiting the dark races. They watched us in World War II as we began a holy war but ended in setting loose the most monstrous of all weapons, so monstrous that, in twenty-five years, only we have used it.

They see us now in Vietnam.

Is it any wonder that we are charged now with genocide? And let us be honest enough to examine that charge as it is used by Stokely Carmichael, Rap Brown, and others. When these men use it, they don't mean simply that America would choose to exterminate physically all people of color, though there is mounting evidence that this is precisely what we will do if we have to.

Let us remember that the charge was first made at the time when the most rapid strides were being taken toward integration, when civil rights legislation was being passed, when presidents and Southern mayors were joining hands and singing "We Shall Overcome." Why do you suppose they talk about genocide? Because it began to be evident to black men what we meant by integration. Black men began to see what Markus Barth had pointed out to us five years ago, that while white, good, liberal Americans were open to the social needs, necessities, and opportunities of the present hour, there was a condition to it. They began to see that we were willing—yes, even eager—to receive blacks into *our* schools, *our* neighborhoods, *our* jobs, *our* clubs, perhaps *our* churches (sometimes), and even into *our* families and bedrooms. But they also saw that our understanding of the end of segregation was usually identified with that kind of acceptance which presupposes, among other things, that there are two cultures, two races, two types of men, a hierarchy of creation. "Integration" came to mean actively pursuing a course that allowed the two races to encounter each other in such a way that the white partner could forgive his black brother for being black and permit him to become an honorary white man. Nothing more was required of blacks other than that they learn their lessons: keep their yards clean, keep their voices down, wash themselves at least once a day, enjoy the treasures of higher culture, stabilize their courtship and marriage customs, just as the white man is alleged to have done. The beginning of genocide is not ovens and concentration camps. The beginning of genocide is the beginning of integration: the expectation of the majority that the minority will become like the majority.

What we tried to peddle was racial migration, and we failed to sell it. We failed because it was a faulty commodity. It was no more than segregation turned inside out. And the first faint cry of black power scared us so badly that we quickly, immediately, distorted it to mean not what it originally did mean—namely, the development of political movements capable of securing just demands as other American minorities have done. We distorted black power to mean what white power has meant all these centuries—a ruthless ruling by the powerful of the powerless. Thus we stand as failures because we deserve to have failed.

* * *

We have failed on the racial front in the second place because *every* institution of our culture has found a way out of meeting the crisis. The sin of the responsible institutions of culture is not that they have lied, but that they have carefully and cunningly manipulated the truth—each with its own shibboleth, each with its own idol. The god of the racist is racial supremacy. But we were smart enough and good enough to isolate that. Grant him his premise, and you cannot beat him. We rightly identified his grave sin as idolatry. But we did not realize that in the process we were creating our own idol and idols. One idol after another was brought into play, which, in effect, excused us of any real responsibility.

American industry today argues for and hides behind the false god of "merit employment." Let's give them a test. Those who make the highest score will get the job. Guess who gets the job? The tests are written by people who for the most part know about pheasant-under-glass. If you ask some ghetto child about pheasant-under-glass, he makes zero. But ask him about the breeding habits of cockroaches or how a rat can crawl up an iron crib and gnaw the toes and fingers off his baby sister, and he will make a good grade while the middle-class applicant will make zero.

Another example is the American press with its idol of objectivity. The importance of fair and impartial coverage of the news is valid. But it is not enough in this day of national peril simply to react to, report, and shoot pictures of the various crises. In wartime, the press is always filled with pages of patriotic slogans designed to support the leadership in an emergency. The press does not hesitate to propagandize for other good causes—the United Fund, the Boy Scouts, National Science Week. But when it comes to the human situation of *race* (though there are notable exceptions), the press is piously faithful to the cult of objectivity and sends this great tragedy back to the racist, white and black, to be solved.

Another example is the church in America with its concern for peace and harmony within the fellowship—a valid concept, no doubt, until we consider that the man whom many of us call "Lord" used the church primarily as a place to raise hell.

Another example is "education." The American colleges and universities (Christian and otherwise) have carefully avoided any involvement in the racial crisis by worshiping at the shrine of academic excellence. The president of a great Southern university remarked to us a few years ago, once it had been decided, after all that time, to admit five or six *qualified black students* and we had been summoned by someone other than the president to serve as "consultants" to the situation: "We don't contemplate any problem here because there won't be many to measure up to our high standards." He spoke the truth. In this way higher education washes its hands pure in the Pilate basin of academic excellence and sends the problem back to the racist, black and white. But it is doubtful that the shibboleth of academic standards is ultimately any more sacred to God than the hue and cry of racial intermarriage—the shibboleth of the deep South racist—is sacred to God. Both, no doubt, contain an element of some sort of "truth": both are worshiping false gods.

* * *

The failure of education requires a closer look at dimensions that include, but go beyond, the racial one. An important reason why the racial catastrophe is deep and probably irreversible is what America now means by and does with "education." Education's failure, together with the perversion of education that came about in the process of failing the racial crisis, is probably the most monumental calamity to befall an institution of American culture in the twentieth century. The refusal "to bus" in order to achieve some degree of balance leading toward an effective primary and secondary educational process, and the failure of higher education to seek out in order to serve the victims of this process, are simply the two most obvious manifestations of the same calamity.

We are concerned here, however, with the failure of education that falls as an especially acute judgment on the Christian in America. The New Testament proclaims the Good News that religion—that sickness which binds man to himself and to his idols and images—is conquered by the resurrection. What concerns us is the fact that "education" has become a religion in the American democracy (and to the church) more sacred than democracy itself (and Christ). The New Testament makes it clear that "education" is not "evangelism." What concerns us is the fact that the gamut of activities that goes by the name "education"—that activity which was to be the sure and certain guarantee that the American people would become free and continue to live in freedom and democracy—along with and urgently supported by the political order, is preparing our minds and souls for the technological concentration camp.

We are concerned about more than a virtue that has become a vice, a thesis that has become an antithesis, a tragedy that is more than intellectual because it involves the souls of the humanists and the birthright of Christians. We are convinced, for example, that the gut decisions that Christians will face in the next years and decades will not primarily concern military service (it is more efficient to have a voluntary, professional army) but rather service to the idol of American "education." We believe that Christians will soon be forced to make decisions about whether to permit their children to attend institutions (from kindergarten upward, Christian and secular), spawned by educational systems and bureaucracies that are already hopelessly closed, totalitarian, and beyond hope of internal or external renewal, and whose efforts produce a generation of youth either cynical because of the manifest hypocrisy or brainwashed as to value and meaning in life. And Christians must make those decisions—like all decisions made as Christians—in the light of the fact that it is the Good News, and not "education," which liberates captives from the dungeons of idolatry.

Christians are more confused than anyone today about what "education" *is*. Or perhaps most Christians are not confused, but rather naively assume that they know what education *is*—and that, today, is to be far, far worse off than to be confused. The real charge that must be leveled against Christians is that it was not we, but the plethora of revolts by blacks, youth, police, Indians, etc., which challenged all our easy, liberal assumptions about what "education" *is*. Is education, for example, the objective transmission of information, data, facts, and skills about sundry subjects, liberating the recipient from ignorance about certain information, data, facts, skills—so that choices may be made on the basis of "reason," and every choice made by those receiving this information, data, etc., is thereby "rational"? Perhaps so. But who decides what information, data, facts, and skills will be transmitted, and by whom, and why can we trust one person's objectivity and reject another's as subjective and emotional?

Or is education the appreciation of cultural, especially Western, traditions, enabling one to better understand the world and the time in which we live? Perhaps so. But who decides how to present *what* about *which* tradition? For example, shall we agonize and assign term papers about the "meaning" of the Protestant Reformation and the Age of Reason, and thus ignore the "meaning" of the introduction of the traffic in black lives from Africa to the "new" world by white Christian ladies and gentlemen? Shall we chart the battle of New Orleans and Gettysburg, and thus deny Christian genocide against the original inhabitants of what we now call North and Central and South America? Shall we memorize Talcott Parson's theory of social action and overlook J. Edgar Hoover's?

Some believe that education is the great equalizer in

American democracy. Accessible to all regardless of race, creed, and color, it is the one sure vehicle that permits a son or daughter of a black mother and white father to attend public schools anywhere without prejudice or impediment, secure admission into the crack universities or Christian liberal arts colleges, and become Abraham Lincoln, Richard Nixon, Betty Furness, Jonas Salk, or Neil Armstrong. The fact is that tax-supported education (and *all* education, some Baptists and others to the contrary notwithstanding, *is* tax-supported) aids upper- and middle-income children far more than it supports these lower-income folk. Indeed, these folk—because of who they are and what America has done to them and where they live—are the victims of the very educational system that their own tax dollars support in a higher proportion than do upper- and middle-income families. This fact we hereby commend to the earnest consideration of trustees in the small Christian college who are concerned about the separation of church and state, government support, etc.—not that they accept government support, but that they recognize an indebtedness to those who support *them*. And what about the black man's blackness, the red man's redness, etc., in education today? It is a "problem" that requires a "solution": those who are different because of skin color or "cultural deprivation" are made into "white"—in public institutions under the rubric of democracy, in Christian institutions under the rubric of brotherhood.

Some hold to a robust American pragmatism: we know what education is when we see what it does. On that score, also, we question an easy assurance. Education in the United States has studied war and the decision-making and political processes and power politics so thoroughly since World War II that a class of American mandarins has been created by our graduate schools. But this educational process, itself an object of critical professional inquiry only very recently (that is, after the barn

had burned with the horses inside) has offered no alternative to the cold war, to worldwide insurrections of race
and poverty, to an understanding of the Middle Eastern
crises that are surely wrenching Hitler's victims there into
his own violent image, and that not without racial
touches. As for Vietnam, it is the crown jewel of those
scientists of human affairs (especially political affairs)
who reject even the moral judgments of humanity as
weak and subjective intrusions into the world of political
realism.

Education today might well be judged by what it does.
And what we see it doing is adjusting the student to "the
system" which is everywhere. In other words, it is dehumanizing the student rather than liberating him. Education should work toward an adjustment of "the system"
which is to serve humanity. But because education today
is an adjustment of the student to the system, the great
people and the great literature and the great music and
the great art since World War II have not been the work
of those who are a part of the educational institutions in
America. How could they be? And because this is so, our
educational institutions are prisoners of the manifold
fruits of a technology which the helpless and impoverished of the world and our land know only too well, from
Hiroshima to Hanoi, from Canton in Mississippi to Ocean
Hill-Brownsville in New York. And because this is so,
education, wherever it might take place, must begin as a
process of *dis*-adjustment to "the system." And *that*,
brothers and sisters, is about all we know of what "education" *is* today.

* * *

What are the Christian colleges in all of this? Where
they have always been, led by Caesar and his educational
institutions and bureaucracies, except that, in most cases,
we were early to segregate racially, in order to be relevant

to our people, and late to desegregate because we had to preserve "unity"; and because of the strength of our conviction that our intentions are of the highest and purest quality, we are the last to understand that integration is, in fact, another way to control "them."

Whom does the Christian college serve? Whom do Caesar's colleges serve? The same people, and precious few others. Certainly not the victims of Caesar's educational Gestapos, for these are "high risk." And no one (Caesar's servants or Christ's) gives any thought to how high the risk *any* student runs by devoting four irretrievable years of his life to the sickness of present-day educational establishments. Certainly there is little enthusiasm in the Christian colleges today to resurrect those of whom Jonathan Kozol speaks in *Death at an Early Age*. For which among the present-day colleges has been more anxious about the dodges and deceits called "quality education" and "academic excellence" than the Christian liberal arts college? Which among them has been more anxious about accreditation than the Christian liberal arts college, even though it meant a service to Caesar and a denial of the service to Christ? Which among the educational institutions has competed more enthusiastically and energetically with Caesar for high-quality students (so as not "to scrape the bottom of the barrel"), and for basketball players, faculty, coaches, science centers, and athletic stadiums, than the Christian liberal arts college? Which among the colleges has ignored more effectively than the Christian liberal arts college the stranger lying bloody in the ditch (cf. Luke 10:29ff.), the victim of the very educational system which now denies him?

Whom does the Christian liberal arts college serve when it echoes Caesar's concerns about "qualifications," academic standards, SAT and CEEB and GRE scores? In whose service is the Christian liberal arts college when it fails to strike head-on the very concept of "qualification," especially qualifications defined by the educational brigands who consigned the victim, bruised, naked, and half-dead, into the sewers of American society, dug in part by the educational brigands themselves? Whom does the Christian liberal arts college serve when it does not lead an onslaught against the totalitarianism of accrediting agencies? Where is the Christian liberal arts college which has compassion even on her own victims as well as Caesar's by pouring on oil (and, yes, wine) and paying the bill, not in reparations but as a neighbor.

What we are asking is: Where in the Christian college is the white youngster we call a "Kluxer" because he doesn't know which side of the plate the salad fork goes on and spends a lot of time talking about sex and automobiles? Where in the Christian college is the black whom we call "culturally deprived" and thus ineligible for admission to higher education because he has been deprived (or spared) *our* culture and belches or crepitates in public?

(Let none think, however, that our questions have already been given answers by the Bob Jones-Oral Roberts University types. We have other questions for them, centering around their own capitulation to the techniques of contemporary totalitarianism. The fact is that a few, but not many, of our readers are inheritors of the Bob Jones traditions. A great many of us are debtors to the Christian liberal arts colleges.)

Our Christian colleges speak for mammon, not God. There is precious little evidence that they—that is, their trustees or administrators or faculties or alumni or students—desire the humility to do otherwise than be an agent of mammon. Against what we are saying it may be argued that the Christian liberal arts college is serving Christians—or at least the progeny of Christians—in America. But when was the principal service to Christ ever the rendering of service to ourselves (cf. Luke 10:29ff.)? In our Christian colleges we are in fact serving ourselves and not Christ, in the middle- and upper-income orientation of our curriculum and faculty and administration and trustees. Our distaste for the victims of our economics is never more evident than in our loud shouts about how many more "Negroes," how many more "high-risk" students we admitted than last year, how many more than the state university, how many more than the Ivy League colleges. If we were in the least bit serious about black and high-risk students, why would we have to say anything about *them?* Why not, like the man in Luke 10:29ff., *be* compassionate by binding up wounds and paying the bills and leaving, incognito?

Christian colleges, unlike the medieval universities we like to deplore so much because of their authoritarianism, are contemptuous toward their environments—human and natural—which are exploited rather than served. Christian colleges have constructed buildings and obtained operational capital from a rape of the land and from the sweat and backs of Indians, blacks, rednecks, hillbillies, Kluxers, Chicanos, peckerwoods, etc. The Christian colleges then use them as service or maintenance lackeys, while their pathetic little "culture"-starved M.A.'s and Ph.D.'s ridicule and scoff them and their music and dress and antics and drinking and fighting and sex life and prose and vocabulary and support of George Wallace, and tell lies about them (and thereby about middle- and upper-income Americans and Christians) in their "required" courses.

Our Christian colleges serve themselves and not Christ when they explain in the most pained tones that they have only so "many" resources and that these must be allocated on the basis of priorities. And what and who are the priorities? Ourselves. Middle- and upper-income Christian Americans. And these are the priorities set by Caesar, not by Christ. They are, the Christian colleges insist, committed to "quality education." Spelled out, this means that our Christian colleges will continue their commitment to the very same cycle of events which put and keeps the victims of the educational system, bloodied and bruised and half-dead, in the sewer of American society. And because he smells badly since he has been there so long, the Christian liberal arts college covers the victim not with oil and wine and compassion, but with surveys, institutional self-studies, statements of purpose and massive foundation requests (that were rejected). An allocation of resources based on commitments to "quality education" is simply the educator's "white" lie that a commitment to the victims of the educational system in America is a compromise of "quality education." And this is quite simply the racism of white intransigence, which feeds on the very same conviction of superiority that crucified Christ and recrucifies him anew.

Christ have mercy on us! What is the *quality* of "quality education" that rejects Christ's own dying for *all* men? Where is the quality in what our Christian colleges have taught about what Christian white people have done in wars and slavery to the people of color the world over, and what we have done in our own peculiar wars against each other? Where is the *excellence* that judges it "excellent" to allocate resources to support and preserve the very institutions and ways of life that raped a people and a land and imported the children of God as draft animals, that digs new sewers in which to throw the new victims created by the new systems and methods and techniques of the American way of life?

Where is the service to Christ in that myriad of Christian liberal arts colleges whose only boast over the hated (because of the larger budget) state university is the lower student-teacher ratio (which never really works out to smaller classes in a meaningful way), easy access to the teachers, and the absence of student-faculty radicalism and hippie types? There is *no* service to Christ in all this, for the simple reason that there is no essential difference between what is happening on the campus of the Christian liberal arts college and that of the large state university. Using the same formulas, both compete in recruiting the same students, for the same curriculum, taught by instructors indoctrinated by the same prejudices of the same professors in the same graduate and professional schools—except that instructors at the state universities were, for the most part, better all-round students, have stronger and more realistic and relevant views of today's society, and (unbelievable as it might seem) are on the whole better classroom teachers. (What is the sense in bragging about smaller classes if the students are presided over by imperialistic old maids, male and female?)

So there it is: Students sharing the same presuppositions because they must have them to finish high school and be "admitted" to college; faculty sharing the same ones because they have to get a "degree" and an "appointment" and tenure, promotions, and sabbaticals; administrators sharing them because they have to allocate resources according to the priorities set by society and by Caesar's universities, and by trustees drawn from the specialists in making and raising money in the American system. There they are: the Christian college and the state university, together and indistinguishable, not under the cross but under the great yum-yum tree of academic excellence and quality education. There are no distinctions between "education" and "evangelism" wrought on the cross, but rather the "cross" in the "classroom" and not on Golgotha—evangelism in the service and at the beck and call of education-as-adjustment to the system which is all around us.

But why should we emphasize failures only? Why not, for a change, speak of successes? Because there are no successes. Because insofar as the Christian college is concerned, there will be no successes, absolutely not one, unless and until the nature and the depth of the failure are seen and accepted. And this lies not in our hands, but in God's. We are under his judgment.

It is clear that there will be no successes until the Christian college grasps the difference between teaching and evangelism as seen in the New Testament. Then it will cease evangelizing education by the cheap trick of trying to put "Christ in the classroom." Look for success, then, not in Christian colleges because they call themselves Christian. Look for success in a student here, a "call to discipleship" yonder, an insight there from a teacher which makes it impossible to "study" war or racism or the New Testament and come away the same person, impossible to study physics or chemistry and not dedicate one's career to opposing their enslavement to the horrors of twentieth-century technological inhumanity, impossible to study money and banking and come away lighthearted at what our economics have done to those who originally had property rights to the land which supports us so richly, and to those whom we purchased as chattel and continue to treat as such. Look for success not where "Christ," but a Socratic Christian, is in the classroom—that is, a teacher who will put *everything* under question and accept *nothing* at face value (especially himself and his discipline), not for the hell of it or because he is possessed of a demon, but because the cross and the resurrection put *everything* under question. Yesterday, today, forever. *Everything.*

Look for success in those places, for not under any circumstance is it essential that this kind of success occur only on the campus or in the classroom of the Christian liberal arts college. *That is the point.*

And that is why we speak of failure.

* * *

We wish, finally, to talk about another failure, the failure of the church and society to distinguish between the so-called black problem and the problem of the poor whites. Our nation has refused to see this distinction, we suspect, partly because of our accumulated guilt and partly because we assumed that liberals romanticized the racial problem and sought to identify with the civil rights movement either by ignoring the poor white or by seeing movements, which manifest themselves most often in such groups as the Ku Klux Klan, as a police problem, pure and simple.

A few years ago the Columbia Broadcasting System did a documentary film called "The Ku Klux Klan: An Invisible Empire." It showed the horror of such things as the murder of Goodman, Chaney, and Schwerner in Mississippi, the castration of Judge Aaron in Alabama, and the murder of four Sunday school children in Birmingham. Who would deny that they were dreadful crimes? But, as always, there were many important things which were not put before the audience, most important being the conditions which produced these people. The same thing produced them that produces—and is producing and will produce—more violence in the black ghetto. These same things are producing the white ghettos and will produce the violence, the rioting, and all the rest.

The film did not tell about a friend of ours who is a leader in the Ku Klux Klan. It did not tell about how his father left him when he was six years old or how his mother went to work in a textile sweat shop, where for thirty-seven years her job was to sew the seam down the right leg of overalls. The *outside* right leg, for thirty-seven years—never the inside of the right leg, never the left leg; her job for thirty-seven years was to make the seam down the right side of the overalls, and that was for forty cents an hour, and generally for not more than two days a week. They did not tell us about how this boy ran away, joined the Army at fourteen, was jumping out of airplanes as a paratrooper when he was sixteen and was leading a platoon when he was eighteen. The film didn't tell how for seventeen years he learned the fine arts of torture, interrogation and guerrilla warfare.

The film said that only the Ku Klux Klan has a record of violence as an organization. What of the textile industry sweat shops? What of the American Legion? (What of us—and how much do you pay your maid or your maintenance personnel? How many hungry children are there in your town tonight?)

The film did not tell us that the same social forces producing the Klan's violence produced the violence of Watts, Rochester, Harlem, Cleveland, Chicago, Dayton, Tampa, Houston, Atlanta, Baton Rouge, and Nashville. The Klansmen are of the same stuff, victims of the same social isolation, deprivation economic conditions, rejections, underemployment and unemployment, broken homes, working mothers, ignorance, poor schools, no hospitals, bad diets, and all the rest. Does one have to wonder why the film did not tell us?

The invisible empire? Yes, there is an invisible empire in America, but it is not the Ku Klux Klan.

There is a film of an invisible empire which needs to be made. It should be of the evil and cynical white aristocracy, the few, not in the South but in America, who profited from the sale of human flesh. It should include those who tried to do something about their plight in the Populist movement and the Farmers' Alliance in the 1890s. It should report how the poor, ignorant rednecks were told that if they persisted in their egalitarian activities, their daughters would be ravished *en masse* by blacks. Then the camera should be turned slightly to the northeast, to the little city of Springfield, Massachusetts, where can be found what is said to be the richest street in the world, built not with Yankee ingenuity, but with the sale of rum and slaves. Let there be a few frames for a beautiful upper-class church edifice there, and for its pastor who several years ago said at a very fashionable luncheon that his most annoying problem was one usher who insisted on walking down the aisle in the offering procession in a gray flannel suit instead of the traditional morning cutaway which the other five ushers wore. Let that portion of the film conclude with this same pastor asking of a fellow clergyman from the South in all seriousness, "Do you think the churches of the South will ever wake up and do something about this race problem?"

And if it is to be a film on the invisible empire, then let the electronic devices turn to the political processes in this country, from the capitol dome to the courts, the police stations, the banks, and the savings and loan companies. They are all run not by Kluxers, but by people of the middle and upper incomes, all of them respectable and responsible citizens. And then do not forget again the universities (Christian and otherwise) which—at best, insofar as blacks and other minorities are concerned—recruit those whose cultures and manners are already white, and which, where poor whites are concerned, use their intellect and influence to convince this country's people that those who can't afford to go to or qualify for college should be the ones to go and fight this nation's wars, so that those who can afford to go to college can remain in the safety and security of the ivory towers. Finally, film those rejects of the intellectuals as they are taught to hate and kill and burn and interrogate and torture in the fine art of guerrilla warfare. Film them as they come back home and try to get an even break with the college educated. Watch them as they try to get back into "decent society." Document it with some words of President Johnson a few years ago when he pointed his long, bony finger at the millions in his television audience and said to the Klan, "Get out of the Klan and back into decent society while there is still time"—a remark which rings loudly of a police state. Watch the door as it slams shut in his face. Where else can he go but to the Klan? Who else will have him? Who else wants a boy who was a big somebody in uniform but who is nobody's darling now? And yes, give some footage to the churches which have taught him racism in one way or another from the day he was born—all very decently, all very respectably, all for very good reasons—to preserve the harmony (that is, the wealth) of the institution.

Then let us talk about those who run this invisible empire—the ones who created the Klan and Harlem and Watts and southside Chicago. We will show you an invisible empire that intervenes in an Asian civil war, an invisible empire that calculates exactly the amount of civil rights legislation that can be passed in this country without the white voting backlash becoming a reality, an invisible empire that deprives this country of an adequate health program and a guaranteed annual income so that no child in this rich land, be he Kluxer or Black Nationalist, must go hungry, uneducated, and uncared-for medically.

We are not talking about hating the rich. We are simply saying that the invisible empire in this country is far more subtle, far more insidious, cunning, and treacherous than a few hundred people gathered in a cow pasture around a burning cross. It has *always* been against the law to dynamite churches and burn houses and shoot housewives on public highways. Why then all the HUAC investigations of a group of folks in the deep South? Why indeed? Because what HUAC represents has always been pitted against Southern rednecks. Because we like to simplify problems. We like to find the Jonah and throw him overboard, assured that everything will then be all right.

In the beginning of our history we called ourselves the American "experiment." So did Abe Lincoln. We still do. It was a new and novel idea. As in any experiment, however, it is necessary from time to time to evaluate the data. Any scientist periodically will take a look at what he is doing, make changes, and start all over. Perhaps that time has now come in our history.

Whatever the reasons for our failure, however, let us turn briefly to the consequences. And the most glaring and obvious consequence, it seems to us, is that we are moving rapidly toward a contemporary police state. But we must be careful about that phrase. The images of an "American Hitler" or "Stalin" usually come to mind, with exiles, barbed-wire concentration camps, midnight knocks on the door, edicts suspending the Congress, judiciary and Constitution, the rounding up of potential enemies of the State, and government by the super-generals in the Pentagon and HEW technicians, presided over by the former Chief-of-Staff and the Vice President of the regime that was overthrown. But there is no need for that sort of thing. It is mainly a figment of the liberal's anomie, or the *Schadenfreude* of their money-raisers after they lose elections—not to George Wallace or General Edwin Walker, but to one equally as "liberal" as their own candidate.

We have argued for years that this is *not* the way it is going. The danger is not an American "Hitler," or even an American "Stalin" or "Mao." Such a one would fail for the same reason that Goliath failed against David. We are too cunning, too realistic, too educated, to permit the Goliath of an American Hitler to prevail over us. We would always have enough education to identify Goliath. We could always storm the concentration camps. We could always give our bodies to be burned as we chanted "Freedom! Freedom!"

The opportunity for that sort of martyrdom will be denied us in the technological concentration camp of our era and heritage. William Faulkner had a notion of it when he wrote about our white forefathers coming to these lands "not to escape from tyranny as they claimed and believed, but to establish one." *Ours.* Our tyranny. All quite fitting, proper, legal and democratic—and tech-nological. For the concentration camps we are creating in

this country are going up along the lines we have already
suggested: A little rioting last summer. A little less this
summer. Put it down quietly and quickly. Get better
weapons—an armored personnel carrier and lots of gas.
Establish better central communications. Work out pacts
with the police, fire departments, and National Guards of
sister states. Use computers. A policeman is killed in
Nashville or Los Angeles, and authorities say that Black
Power is responsible. Raid their offices and their homes.
So what if the courts under prodding from the ACLU say
that it was "illegal." Let them redo what has already been
destroyed or burned. Let the judges come down and stop
the next raid with their pieces of paper: we are Law, too.
Pick up blacks with Afro cuts and say they looked like
Eldridge (or Kathleen) Cleaver or Rap Brown or Stokely
Carmichael. Then just pick up blacks, or Chicanos. A
leader disappears in Chicago; another disappears in Waycross, Georgia—not to be heard from again, and nowhere
for the family to go for help. But this is the exception, so
that it will never be reported by NBC News or studied by
the American Political Science Association, since there
were not enough facts for generalization. People become
distrustful. They look suspiciously at everyone in the
dime store and supermarket and cocktail lounge: maybe
he belongs to Black Power; maybe he works for the
police or FBI. Any incident is quickly put down because
American technology and foreign policy are spawning a
nice and successful industry in newer gadgets for people-
control. Try them out to see if they work. Only a few
were killed. We can now spray ten square blocks with
glue, sticking everyone together, or pour a sort of liquid
banana peeling on the streets, or drop a plastic balloon
from a helicopter—they can't burn and loot then! No
riots now. Moreover, it would be a very amusing and
educational sight, the knowledgeable but objective and
impersonal Walter Cronkite giving TV explanations of the
workings of these newest technological miracles: ten

square blocks of people squirming and twisting and wiggling and falling, trying to get out. Very funny—unless you are an old woman, or a baby, or unless such an experience left a trauma on your soul that caused you to wake up screaming about it from a padded cell years hence. Of course, TV news cannot be expected to cover such individual matters. But there will be few killed; indeed, the number of fatalities will be liberally reduced if not wholly eliminated.

* * *

Riding south of the city of Chicago a couple of summers ago, we were shown by our host all the magnificent new housing developments, with mile after mile of highrise apartments. "Look at that one," he explained enthusiastically. "The children never have to go outside! A school and a supermarket are inside there. A doctor is there. A hospital is there. A church. They *never* have to go outside!"

How in God's name can you riot there? You can control half a million people with the turn of a master key, held by a democratically elected official. No killings. No riots. Everything goes merrily on its usual way. Law and order. We are in that concentration camp, and the mark of its efficiency is that we don't know we're in it, for how could anyone willingly and freely commit himself to a concentration camp? We only did what had to be done. But, after all, we made the decisions, for we voted in the progressives and supported their programs. We are members of—or at least vote for—one of the two parties which turn the switches and roll the dials and feed the computers. We studied the political processes in required college courses and learned about our world come-of-age from the religion teachers. We read *The Gospel According to Peanuts.* Thus we know we are where we are because of our own free, democratic choices. There are no concentration camps here, no barbed wire, no sadistic guards making us perform unspeakable acts, no camp adminis-trators stretching tattooed human flesh over lampshade frames, no ovens stoked with human bodies, no numbers burned on our forearms, no Anne Frank or Dietrich Bonhoeffer or Heinrich Himmler or Joseph Goebbels. We are free because we did only what had to be done. And if we did it, are we not then free?

* * *

If that is what is coming, why go on? Why do we go on trying? Well, we don't go on trying. Trying is not what we must do. We go on not because of our ideals, but because of what God did for us in Christ. We go on because of St. Paul's imperative: "Be reconciled!" *Katal-lagete!* Be what you are. Be what God's new creation in Christ has made you. We do not go on in the name of social action, for social action negates, turns away from, denies God's new creation in Christ.

We cannot make an order out of an idea. However, we can participate in the order already made, not by us, but for us—for all of us—in Christ.